In the name of Allāh, Most Gracious, Most Merciful. All praise is due to Allāh, the Lord of the worlds. And peace, blessings and salutations be upon His Prophet, Nabī Muḥammad ﷺ .

Pearls from the Path

A Collection of Anecdotes and Stories from Islamic History.

Volume Three

Compiled by
Moulānā Afzal Ismail

First Edition Dhul Ḥijjah 1432 / November 2011

Published by:
Muslims at Work
P.O. Box 606, Heidelberg, 1438
South Africa

ISBN 978-0-620-51850-5

Distributed by:
Muslims at Work
Website : www.matwork.co.za
Email : info@muslimsatwork.co.za
Tel : +27 73 183 0721

Distributor for Europe:
Azhar Academy Ltd
www.azharacademy.com
sales@azharacademy.com
54-68 Little Ilford Lane - Manor Park - London E12 5QA
Tel. +44 (0) 20 8911 9797 - Fax. +44 (0) 20 8911 8999

Printed in Turkey by Mega Printing
export@mega.com.tr

لَقَدْ كَانَ فِي قَصَصِهِمْ عِبْرَةٌ لِأُولِي الْأَلْبَابِ

Indeed, in their stories there is a lesson

for men of understanding.

- Sūrah Yūsuf, verse 111

Transliteration Key

أ إ - ’
ا آ - ā
ب - b
ت - t
ث - th
ج - j
ح - ḥ
خ - kh
د - d
ذ - dh
ر - r
ز - z
س - s
ش - sh
ص - ṣ
ض - ḍ
ط - ṭ
ظ - ẓ
ع - ‘, ‘a, ‘i, ‘u
غ - gh
ف - f
ق - q
ك - k
ل - l
م - m
ن - n
و - ū
ه - h
ي - y, ī

﷾ - Used after the name of Allāh, translated as, “Praise be to Allāh Who is pure and elevated.”

ﷺ - Used after the name of Nabī Muḥammad ﷺ, translated as, “May Allāh’s peace and blessing be upon him.”

﵇ - Used after the name of a prophet of Allāh, translated as, “May Allāh’s peace be upon him.”

﵁, ﵂ - Used after the name of a Ṣaḥābī (companion) of Nabī Muḥammad ﷺ, translated as, “May Allāh be pleased with him / her.”

﵃ - Used after the names of more than one Ṣaḥābī (companion) of Nabī Muḥammad ﷺ, translated as, “May Allāh be pleased with them.”

رحمها الله, ﵀ - Used after the name of a pious person, translated as, “May Allāh’s mercy be upon him / her.”

Contents

Foreword

by Mufti Siraj Desai
Principal of Darul-Uloom Abu Bakr, Port Elizabeth

In The Name of Allāh, Most Gracious, Most Merciful. Special Salāt and Salām be upon Our Master Hazrat Muḥammad ﷺ, upon his family and his illustrious companions and descendants.

I have had the good fortune of reading through some sections of the book *Pearls of the Path* compiled by Moulana Afzal Ismail Sahib. Māshā-Allāh, the book makes for extremely interesting reading. It is well written and ideally designed, and the short moral that follows each anecdote provides the reader with a quick, practical lesson that could be implemented in one's day-to-day life. I am sure this anthology of anecdotes will go a long way towards creating some awareness in readers with regard to good character, compassion, respect, humility, and all the various themes it comprises.

Readers should also appreciate the fact that this book was compiled from a wide selection of classical and authentic Arabic and Urdu works, making it a sound source of reference as well. May Allāh ﷻ reward the writer and the publishers for this very commendable effort, and make it a means of guidance for all who read it, āmīn.

Humbly yours,

Siraj Desai
Port Elizabeth
15 Dhul-Ḥijjah 1432
11 November 2011

Preface

All praise belongs to Allāh ﷻ, the Creator, Nourisher and Sustainer of the universe. Peace, blessings and salutations be upon the best of Allāh's ﷻ creation, our master and leader, Nabī ﷺ.

The illustrious writer and scholar, Ibn Jawzī رحمه الله, while explaining the relevance of the stories of the pious, mentioned,

انها دليل السالك و قوت الطالب و بها تقوي نفوس المريدين

"Stories serve as a guide for the one who treads the path of spirituality, and are a form of nourishment for the seeker. By means of stories the souls of the disciples find strength."

The renowned sage, Mālik ibn Dīnār رحمه الله aptly stated,

الحكايات تحف الجنة

"Stories are the gifts of paradise."[1]

With the help of Allah ﷻ, volume three of Pearls from the Path has been completed. An earnest attempt has been made to trace each of the narrations from authentic Arabic sources. Where an incident is narrated in multiple sources, the first reference has been mentioned in full.

I wish to express my sincere gratitude to all those who assisted in the project; Mufti Husain Kadodia for perusing the manuscript and offering valuable feedback; Molānā Yusuf Abba and Younus Ismail for the proof-reading; my wife for her encouragement and ideas. May Allāh ﷻ reward them all abundantly in this world and the Hereafter for rendering their invaluable assistance towards the accomplishment of this project. May Allāh ﷻ accept this truly humble effort and make it a source of salvation for me, my parents, family, teachers and well-wishers.

Afzal Ismail
28 Dhul Qa'dah 1432 / 26 October 2011

---

1 ʿUyūnul Ḥikāyāt, p11

Overlooking the Shortcomings of a Spouse

A man came to ʿUmar ‎ to complain about his wife. As he reached his door, he heard Ummī Kulthūm, ʿUmar's ‎ wife, speaking harshly to him.

The man thought to himself, "I intended to complain about my wife to him, but he appears to be afflicted with the same problem I am experiencing."

He turned around and began to leave. ʿUmar ‎ noticed him leaving and called him back.

When questioned about his visit, he explained, "I came to complain to you about my wife, but I overheard your wife and decided to leave."

ʿUmar ‎ explained, "I have adopted a forgiving nature towards her because of the rights she has upon me. Firstly, she serves as a barrier between me and hell-fire and my heart is contented with her as she saves me from indulging in ḥarām. Secondly, she protects my wealth when I leave my home. Thirdly, she washes my clothes. Fourthly, she attends to the upbringing of my children and fifthly, she cooks and prepares my food."

After hearing this, the man replied, "I enjoy the same benefits from my wife, but I have never overlooked her faults and shortcomings. In future, I shall do so."[1]

One of the secrets of marital bliss and harmony is to focus on the positives of one's spouse and forgive the shortcomings.

1 Ṣafḥātun Rā'idah Fī Masīratil ʿAdālah, p 287; Tambīhul Ghāfilīn

Just Rulers

There was once a ruler in West Africa, who received news about a woman who owned a sugarcane plantation. A single sugarcane reed from her plantation would fill an entire bowl with juice, when extracted. The ruler decided to take possession of the plantation. He visited her and asked whether her sugarcane indeed produced so much juice as people claimed.

She replied, "Yes, it is true."

She then had a reed of sugarcane pressed, but it did not even fill half a bowl.

The ruler asked in astonishment, "What has happened? I was informed otherwise!"

The woman replied, "The news that reached you was correct, but the ruler has made an intention to usurp this land from me. This has removed the *barakah* (blessings)."

The ruler immediately repented and made an intention not to take the land away from her. He then asked her to extract some juice. This time the bowl was filled as usual.[1]

The justice of rulers draws barakah, while oppression invites poverty and grief.

1 Sirājul Mulūk, p 45

Fear the Curse of an Oppressed Person

ʿAmr ibn Dīnār narrates: A man was once walking on the seashore, when he heard a person exclaiming, "I should serve as an example for a person who intends committing an act of oppression." When requested to explain what he meant by this statement, he replied, "I was once a policeman walking on this very shore, when I noticed a fisherman catching a fish. I requested him to give the fish to me, but he refused. I then asked him to sell it to me, but he still refused. I then struck him on the head and forcefully took it away from him.

As I walked away with the fish in my hand, it bit me on my thumb. The wound was small but gradually increased in size. I endeavoured to treat it, but my efforts were in vain. When my thumb had swollen considerably, I decided to consult a doctor. He advised that I had no choice but to amputate my thumb, as the wound would spread to my other limbs. My thumb was then amputated. Soon thereafter, I noticed that my palm had become infected. Again the doctor advised that my only choice was to amputate my hand. I consented, but my woes were not over. The wound then spread to my arm. When I saw this, I dashed out of my home in desperation, screaming like an animal. After wandering about for some time, I decided to rest beneath a large tree and fell asleep. In my dream, a person appeared to me and asked, "How many more of your limbs will be amputated? Rather, seek forgiveness from the person whom you had oppressed and you will be cured."

When I awoke, I realised the truth of the message conveyed in the dream and knew that it was a warning from Allāh to repent from my evil deed. I made my way to the seashore, in search of the fisherman. When I reached him, he was busy removing his fishing net from the water. It contained a large amount of fish. He did not recognise me and asked who I was.

I begged him to forgive me and explained, "I am the policeman who assaulted you and took your fish." I showed him my hand and he immediately recited some words seeking refuge in Allāh from His displeasure. He then forgave me. Immediately, the wound on my arm began to heal. I turned around to leave, but he said to me, "This is not justice in my opinion. I had cursed you for a single fish which would have made no difference to me, and my prayer was accepted." He grasped my hand and led me to his home. When we had entered, he instructed his son to dig up a particular corner of the floor and removed a chest filled with gold coins. His son counted out ten thousand coins and the fisherman handed them to me, saying, "Take this and use it when you need to." He then instructed his son to count out another ten thousand coins and handed them over to me, saying, "Distribute these to your poor relatives and neighbours."

As I was about to depart, I decided to ask him how he had cursed me on that fateful day.

He replied, "When you struck me on the head and snatched my fish, I looked up at the sky and called out: 'O Allāh, You created us both, but You made him strong and me weak. You allowed him to overpower me and due to my weakness I could not oppose him. You did not grant me the strength to prevent his oppression upon me. By the power with which You created him and made him strong and me weak, I beg You to make him an example for humanity.' "[1]

The duʿā' of the oppressed is readily accepted in the Court of Allāh ﷻ, as the veil between the oppressed servant and his Creator is removed.

1 Ar-Rawḍur Rayyāhīn, p 239

Compassion

A person, once, approached a scholar and requested that the pious man teach him the Ismul Aa'ẓam[1].

The scholar asked him, "But, do you consider yourself worthy of it?"

"Yes," the man answered.

The scholar decided to test him and instructed, "Proceed to the gates of the city. Observe what happens very carefully and then report back to me."

The man proceeded and sat down close to the gates of the city. After some time, he noticed an aged wood-cutter with a donkey entering the city with some firewood.

The guard at the gate struck the old man and took the firewood away from him. After witnessing the episode of injustice, the man returned and reported to the scholar what he had observed.

The scholar enquired, "What would you have done to the guard if you had known the Ismul Aa'ẓam?"

The man replied, "I would have prayed for his destruction."

The scholar then explained, "That wood-cutter was the one who taught me the Ismul Aa'ẓam. Only those who have patience, mercy and compassion for creation are worthy of knowing it."[2]

Man often desires power, but does not have the understanding and insight to use it wisely. The wise and intelligent men of Allāh ﷻ know the dangers associated with the abuse of power and take the necessary steps to prevent it.

1 The greatest name of Allāh ﷻ through which Allāh ﷻ fulfils people's needs.

2 Al-I'itibār Min Siyaril Abrār, p120; Fazā'ile Ṣadaqāt

Wealth is a Trial

Imām Shamsuddīn Abū ʿAbdullāh Muḥammad ibn ʿAbdur Raḥīm رحمة الله عليه was a scholar of the Ḥanbalī school of thought. He taught Ḥadīth for forty years and was known for his devotion to knowledge, worship and good deeds. Once, he and his wife were digging at a certain point on Mount Ṣāliḥiyyah for something, when he unearthed a purse filled with dinārs. He immediately covered it with soil, despite their poverty-stricken condition.

He explained to his wife, "This wealth is a trial upon us. Perhaps it belongs to somebody." He then made her promise that she would neither divulge their discovery to anybody nor attempt to search for it again. She was righteous like her husband, and agreed to his proposal.[1]

Wise men recognise the harms of ill-gotten riches.

بسم الله الرحمن الرحيم

Price of Deception

A man was once on a journey and stopped at nightfall at a place notorious for criminals and robbery. He had a large amount of dirhams on him and was naturally afraid of being robbed. He, therefore, approached a man in the neighbourhood, who appeared to be honest, and requested whether he could spend the night at his home. The man agreed.

1 Shadhrātudh Dhahab, vol 7, p 709

When the host realised that the traveller had money on him, he decided to kill and rob him of all his possessions. He put the traveller to sleep in the same room as his young son, who had no idea what his father had planned.

Late that night, when all was quiet, the man extinguished the lamp and approached the bed of the traveller. It so happened, that the traveller and the young boy had swopped beds before retiring. The man thinking that he was at the bedside of the traveller, began to strangle him. The young boy offered no resistance and passed away almost immediately. The traveller was awakened and realised what had happened. He ran out of the house and notified the residents of the neighbourhood. The man was arrested and admitted to the murder of his own son. The traveller was handed back his money and departed as swiftly as he could.[1]

An evil plot often has disastrous consequences upon the perpetrator in addition to the torment that awaits him in the Hereafter.

Duʿā' of the Oppressed

Jābir bin Samurah ﷺ narrates : The people of Kūfah complained to ʿUmar ﷺ about their governor, Saʿd ﷺ. Consequently, ʿUmar ﷺ dismissed him and appointed ʿAmmār ﷺ as their leader. They lodged a variety of complaints against Saʿd ﷺ and even alleged that he did not perform Ṣalāh properly.

ʿUmar ﷺ sent for him and said, "O Abū ʿAffān, these people claim that you do not perform Ṣalāh properly."

1 Al-Faraj Baʿdash Shiddah

He replied, "By Allāh, I perform Ṣalāh with them similar to the Ṣalāh of Nabī ﷺ and I do not exclude anything from it. I prolong the first two rakāts of ʿIshā' Ṣalāh and shorten the last two."

ʿUmar رضي الله عنه said, "O Abū ʿAffān, this is what I expected from you."

He then sent a few people with him to the people of Kūfah to enquire about him. They proceeded and did not leave any Masjid without enquiring from the congregation about him. They all praised him until they arrived at the Masjid of the tribe of Banī ʿAbs.

A man called ʿUsāmah ibn Qatādah, commonly known as Abū Saʿdah, stood up and said, "As you have bound us under an oath, I am obliged to tell you that Saʿd did not accompany the army in battle, nor did he deal justly and distribute the wealth equally amongst us."

Saʿd رضي الله عنه said, "I then supplicated to Allāh ﷻ for three things: 'O Allāh! If Abū Saʿdah is a liar, and has stood up to boast and earn a name for himself, then prolong his life, increase his poverty and afflict him with trials.' "

Later, when Abū Saʿdah was asked how things had turned out for him, he would reply that he was an old man in tribulation, as a result of Saʿd's رضي الله عنه curse. He would be seen loitering in the streets with his eyebrows overhanging his eyes, due to old age.[1]

The duʿā' of an oppressed person is readily accepted by Allāh ﷻ.

1 Bukhārī

بِسْمِ اللهِ الرَّحْمٰنِ الرَّحِيْمِ

Pious Judge Admonishes King

The Khalīf Nāṣir of Andalūs had spent an enormous sum of money in decorating the Madīnatuz Zahrā'. He had plastered the roof and walls with gold and silver. Its roof was a mixture of bright yellow and snow white and so overwhelmingly beautiful, that the light reflected from it would dazzle the sight. One day, as he was seated amongst his courtiers and attendants, admiring the splendour of his efforts, he proudly asked, "Have any of you ever heard of a king before me who constructed a building as magnificent?"

They replied, "No, by Allāh, Amīrul-Mu'minīn. You are unique in this regard. No king in our knowledge ever constructed the likes of what we see here."

Just as he was deriving pleasure and delight from their replies, Judge Mundhir ibn Sa'īd رحمة الله عليه walked in with his head lowered. After he had taken his seat, the Khalīf asked the judge what he thought about the unprecedented splendour of the palace.

Tears began to fall from the judge's eyes onto his beard and he replied, "O Amīrul-Mu'minīn, Allāh ﷻ has granted you many bounties out of His grace and has greatly elevated your status amongst nations. I did not expect you to allow the accursed Shaiṭān to prompt and deceive you in this manner. You have allowed Shaiṭān to degrade you to the status of the disbelievers."

The Khalīf was quite taken aback with this and retorted, "Be careful of what you are saying! How have I reached the level of the disbelievers?"

The judge answered, "Does Allāh ﷻ not say,

وَلَوْلَا أَنْ يَكُوْنَ النَّاسُ أُمَّةً وَاحِدَةً لَجَعَلْنَا لِمَنْ يَكْفُرُ بِالرَّحْمٰنِ لِبُيُوْتِهِمْ سُقُفًا مِنْ فِضَّةٍ
وَمَعَارِجَ عَلَيْهَا يَظْهَرُوْنَ وَلِبُيُوْتِهِمْ أَبْوَابًا وَسُرُرًا عَلَيْهَا يَتَّكِئُوْنَ وَزُخْرُفًا وَإِنْ كُلُّ

ذٰلِكَ لَمَّا مَتَاعُ الْحَيَاةِ الدُّنْيَا وَالْآخِرَةُ عِنْدَ رَبِّكَ لِلْمُتَّقِينَ

'And were it not that all mankind would have become of one community (of disbelievers), We would have provided for those who disbelieve in the Most Beneficent (Allāh), silver roofs for their houses, and stairs (of silver) whereby they ascend, and for their houses, doors (of silver), and thrones (of silver) on which they could recline, and adornments of gold. Yet all this (i.e. the roofs, doors, stairs, thrones and so on) would have been nothing but an enjoyment of this world. And the Hereafter with your Lord is only for the Allāh-fearing.' "(Sūrah Az-Zukhruf, verse 33-35)

The Khalīf was speechless and lowered his head. Fearful of Allāh's ﷻ punishment, tears began to fall from his eyes. After a while, he turned to Judge Mundhir and remarked, "O Judge, may Allāh ﷻ reward you well for your concern. May He bring forth more men like you. You have spoken the truth."

He rose from the gathering, repenting to Allāh ﷻ, and commanded that the gold and silver be removed from the roof of the palace and that it be replastered with sand.[1]

The path of truth is the path of success.

~

The truth should be spoken no matter how bitter and unpalatable it may be to others.

1 Nafḥuṭ Ṭīb Min Ghuṣnil Andalus Ar-Raṭīb, p 573

Qārī Bāsit's رحمة الله عليه Recitation Reduces Communists to Tears

Once Qārī ʿAbdul Bāsit رحمة الله عليه, the famous reciter of the Glorious Qur'ān, was asked, "You recite Qur'ān with a great deal of enthusiasm. Have you ever witnessed any miracle regarding the Qur'ān?"

He replied, "You ask about one miracle. I have personally witnessed many miracles regarding the Qur'ān."

When prompted to relate one such miracle, he explained, "Jamāl ʿAbdun Nāṣar, during his reign as the president of Egypt, once travelled through Russia. Communism was dominant during that period and commanded a great deal of respect globally. Today, Allāh has completely shattered its power and influence through Jihād. In any case, Jamāl ʿAbdun Nāṣar visited Moscow and had state meetings with a number of political figures. After the termination of official proceedings, he would often indulge in casual discussions. During one such gathering, the Communists asked him, "Why do you not study Communism and abandon Islām? If you do so, we will transform your country by introducing the latest and most advanced technology. You will then become the leaders in technological advancement."

Jamāl ʿAbdun Nāṣar responded to them but was constrained to terminate his discussions due to time constraints. He left for Egypt, but felt that he had not done justice in expounding the truth and beauty of Islām. Two years later, he again had the opportunity to visit Russia."

Qārī ʿAbdul Bāsit رحمة الله عليه continues, "I received an official letter from the president requesting me to accompany him on his trip. I was surprised. I would have regarded an invitation to the Arab World, Pakistan or any other Muslim country as normal, but an invitation to Russia was unbelievable. What would I be required to do in a country where people were atheists? In any case, I made preparations and proceeded with the president. After official meetings were over, a portion of time in his schedule was allocated for casual discussions. Jamāl ʿAbdun Nāṣar courageously introduced me to them and requested that I recite for them. They asked what I would recite, and were informed that I would recite a portion of the Qur'ān. I began reciting the portion of Sūrah Ṭahā, which had converted ʿUmar ﷺ to Islām.

طه مَا أَنْزَلْنَا عَلَيْكَ الْقُرْآنَ لِتَشْقَى إِلَّا تَذْكِرَةً لِمَنْ يَخْشَى... إِنَّنِي أَنَا اللهُ لَا إِلَهَ إِلَّا أَنَا فَاعْبُدْنِي وَأَقِمِ الصَّلَاةَ لِذِكْرِي

I recited two rukūs of the Sūrah and upon opening my eyes, I witnessed a miracle of the Qur'ān. Four or five of the Communists, sitting before me, were reduced to tears."

Jamāl ʿAbdun Nāṣar asked them why they were crying and they replied, "We have no idea what your companion has just recited, but the powerful words melted our hearts and caused tears to flow from our eyes. Its effect upon us is beyond explanation."[1]

The immortal words of the Qur'ān have the miraculous effect of softening and conquering the hearts of men.

Forbearance of Nabī ﷺ Converts a Rabbi

Zaid ibn Saʿnah relates: I recognised every sign of prophethood from the face of Nabī ﷺ, except two: his forbearance preceding his ignorance and his ability to respond with greater compassion when encountering an excessive degree of ignorance from another person. I quietly pursued him, eagerly awaiting an opportunity to test his levels of forbearance and ignorance. One day, Nabī ﷺ emerged from his home accompanied by ʿAlī ﷺ when a Bedouin confronted him.

1 Ahle Dil Ke Tarpādene Wāle Wāqiāt, p 409

The Bedouin said, "O Nabī of Allāh, so-and-so tribe has accepted Islām. I informed them that food provisions would reach them soon, as they are in a severe drought. I fear, O Nabī of Allāh, that they may leave Islām just as eagerly as they had accepted it. If you deem it appropriate, please dispatch some provisions to them. Nabī ﷺ turned to his companion, ʿUmar رضي الله عنه, who responded, "We do not have any provisions left."

At this, Zaid ibn Saʿnah continues: I approached him and requested him to sell me a stipulated quantity of dates from the orchard of a particular person after a fixed period of time. Nabī ﷺ agreed to the sale, but did not name the orchard of any person. I then opened my purse and handed him eighty mithqāls of gold as payment for the dates. Nabī ﷺ handed the money over to the Bedouin, saying, "Ensure that provisions reach them quickly."

Zaid ibn Saʿnah says: Two or three days prior to the agreed date of payment, Nabī ﷺ attended the janāzah of an Ansārī. Abū Bakr, ʿUmar, ʿUthmān and a number of other Ṣaḥābah were in his company. After performing the janāzah, he sat down close to a wall. I approached him, grabbed his cloak and stared at him harshly. I then yelled at him, saying, "O Muḥammad, will you not pay what is due to me? I have not known the family of ʿAbdul Muṭṭalib to delay in payment, and I am well aware of your dealings with people."

I turned around to look at ʿUmar. His eyes were angrily turning in their sockets. He looked intently at me and said, "Enemy of Allāh, do you have the audacity of addressing and dealing with the Nabī of Allāh in this manner? By the oath of that Being Who sent him with the truth, had I not feared missing the janāzah, I would have beheaded you with this very sword of mine!"

In the meantime, Nabī ﷺ was looking at ʿUmar calmly. He then said, "ʿUmar, you should have advised in a different manner. You should have advised me to be gracious in payment and him to request his dues kindly. ʿUmar, go and pay him what is due to him and give him twenty Ṣāʿ (a measurement of weight) extra because you threatened him."

ʿUmar accompanied me and paid me what was due to me. He also gave me an extra twenty Ṣāʿ's of dates.

I asked, "What are these extra dates for?"

He replied, "Nabī ﷺ ordered me to give them to you, because I had threatened you."

I asked, "Do you know who I am, O ʿUmar?"

He replied, "No, who are you?"

I replied, "I am Zaid ibn Saʿnah."

He asked, "Are you the famous rabbi?"

I replied, "Yes, I am the rabbi."

In surprise, he asked, "Why did you then address and deal with Nabī ﷺ in such a harsh manner?"

I replied, "O ʿUmar, I recognised every sign of prophethood from the face of Nabī ﷺ, except two: his forbearance preceding his ignorance and, his ability to respond with greater compassion when encountering an excessive degree of ignorance from another person. I have witnessed both of these now and I make you my witness, O ʿUmar, that I am pleased with Allāh as my Lord, Islām as my religion and Muḥammad ﷺ as a prophet. I am amongst the wealthiest people in Madīnah and make you my witness that I have given half of my wealth as charity to the Ummah of Muḥammad ﷺ."

ʿUmar ؓ returned with Zaid ؓ to Nabī ﷺ where he again proclaimed his belief in Allāh and His Nabī ﷺ. He participated in many battles alongside Nabī ﷺ and was finally martyred during battle, bravely fighting the enemy.[1]

Compassion and forbearance are essential ingredients in winning hearts.

1 Sahīh ibn Ḥibbān

بسم الله الرحمن الرحيم

Forbidding Evil with Wisdom

Abul Qāsim Al-Baghawī رحمة الله عليه arrived in Madīnah while on his journey to perform Ḥaj. He was accompanied by Abū Bakr Al-Admī رحمة الله عليه, who was a fine reciter of the Qur'ān. As they entered the blessed precincts of the Masjidun Nabawī, they noticed an old blind man addressing a large group of people. As they listened, they realised that the old man was relating many incidents and narrations which were false and misleading.

Al-Baghawī رحمة الله عليه immediately said, "I must prevent him from continuing."

But, one of his companions advised, "You are not in Baghdād, where people know you and accept your advice. Here, the gathering is large and you are relatively unknown. You would have more success if you advise Abū Bakr Al-Admī رحمة الله عليه to commence reciting from the Qur'ān."

Al-Baghawī رحمة الله عليه agreed with the idea and instructed Abū Bakr Al-Admī رحمة الله عليه to commence reciting. He had not even completed reciting the Isti'ādhah when people began deserting the gathering of the old man to listen to his recitation. Soon the old man had no audience at all and was left with no option but to terminate his address with the words, "This is how bounties are removed."[1]

Evil is easily defeated when challenged with the truth, presented tactfully.

1 Al-Bidāyah Wan Nihāyah, vol 15, p239

Kindness of an Anonymous Stranger

During the time of Sulaimān ibn ʿAbdul Malik, there was a man by the name of Khuzaimah ibn Bishr who was from the tribe of Banū Asʿad. He was well-known for his generosity, kindness and beneficence. His bounties always seemed plentiful and he continued with his generous ways until his provisions were finally exhausted. Those whom he had assisted in times of need, assisted him for a while, but very soon he was left to fend for himself. When it became apparent that people had turned a blind eye to him, he said to his wife, "I have noticed a change of heart from my friends and colleagues. I have decided to isolate myself in my home until death overcomes me." He then locked his doors, sufficing upon the little provisions that he possessed. When these too were exhausted, he was completely helpless and distraught.

It so happened, that ʿIkramah Al-Fayāḍ was the governor of Al-Jazīrah at the time. He was known by the title of Al-Fayāḍ due to his extreme generosity. One day, as he sat amongst his city officials, mention was made of Khuzaimah ibn Bishr. ʿIkramah asked how he was doing and was informed that his condition had deteriorated to the extent that he had isolated himself within his home.

In astonishment, ʿIkramah asked, "Has Khuzaimah ibn Bishr not found a sympathiser or benefactor so that he could have been freed from his pitiable predicament?"

Later that night, ʿIkramah quietly gathered an amount of four thousand dinārs, which he placed in a bag. He then ordered that his horse be saddled and silently left his home, without his wife's knowledge. He rode out accompanied only by a single servant who assisted in carrying the bag of dinārs. As he reached the door of Khuzaimah, he took the bag from the servant and requested him to leave. He proceeded by himself and knocked at the door.

As Khuzaimah opened the door, ʿIkramah advised, "Please utilise this for your needs," and handed him the bag.

Khuzaimah, finding the bag to be quite weighty, dropped it to the ground in order to pursue the anonymous benefactor who had already turned around to leave. Khuzaimah grabbed hold of the reins of his horse and pleaded, "Who are you? May I be sacrificed for you!"

ʿIkramah replied, "I have come to you at this dark hour with the specific intent of remaining anonymous."

Khuzaimah continued, "I refuse to accept your gift, unless you disclose your identity to me."

ʿIkramah finally consented, "I am *Jābir ʿAtharāt Al-Kirām*."

Khuzaimah again asked, "Please tell me more." But, ʿIkramah refused and left.

Khuzaimah picked up the bag and entered his home. He called out to his wife, "Glad tidings! Allāh has brought an end to our suffering. If this bag is filled with money, it will be more than sufficient for us. Quickly, light a lamp!"

"But we do not have the means to light a lamp," she answered. They finally succeeded in opening the bag and found it filled with dinārs.

In the meantime, ʿIkramah returned home only to find his wife frantically searching for him. He informed her that he had gone out by himself to fulfil an errand. She doubted his explanation and began throwing up a tantrum.

When he observed this, he asked, "Why are you going on like this?"

She replied, "This is due to your evil behaviour towards your wife. The Amīr of Al-Jazīrah, quietly leaving his home at the darkest hour of night without the knowledge of his wife, could only be due to another wife or for military purposes."

ʿIkramah explained, "Allāh knows that none of these reasons compelled me to venture out."

But, she continued, "I insist that you inform me why you went out."

He asked whether she would keep it a secret and she agreed. He then explained to her what had transpired that night. Only after hearing his full story, was her heart and mind at ease.

The next morning, Khuzaimah settled all his debts and purchased what he required. He then made preparations to set out and meet the Khalīf Sulaimān ibn ʿAbdul Malik, in Palestine. He received the necessary permission to enter the court of the Khalīf and greeted as he entered. The Khalīf knew him well and asked why he had not visited him for such a long while.

He replied, "Conditions had become difficult for me."

The Khalīf asked, "But, why did you not approach me for assistance?"

"Due to my weakness," Khuzaimah answered.

The Khalīf asked, "Then who assisted you?"

Khuzaimah replied, "I don't know who it was. During the darkness of night, a man knocked at my door and left a bag of money," and related what had transpired.

The Khalīf enquired, "Will you be able to recognise him?"

Khuzaimah replied, "No, as he appeared disguised. The only words he uttered were *'Jābir ʿAtharāt Al-Kirām'*."

Sulaimān ibn ʿAbdul Malik was eager to know who the stranger was and explained that he would reward him if he ever found out his identity. He then appointed Khuzaimah as the new governor of Al-Jazīrah, in place of ʿIkramah Al-Fayāḍ. He stipulated for him a lucrative salary and ordered him to proceed to Al-Jazīrah without delay.

As Khuzaimah approached the city, ʿIkramah and a number of senior officials emerged to welcome him. They entered the city together. Khuzaimah settled in the state-residence and ordered ʿIkramah to provide full records of the finances while he was governor. It soon became evident that ʿIkramah had spent well beyond his authority. ʿIkramah was asked to reimburse the funds, but failed to do so. He was imprisoned and Khuzaimah insisted that the excess money be repaid.

ʿIkramah explained, "I am not one who safeguards his wealth at the expense of his honour. You may do with me as you please."

Khuzaimah instructed that he be heavily chained and placed in solitary confinement. ʿIkramah remained in this condition for a month, during which time his health deteriorated due to his adverse circumstances.

News of his deteriorating condition reached his wife and she was gravely saddened. She called one of her intelligent and trusted servants and instructed, "Proceed to the governor and request to speak to him privately as you have an important message to convey to him. When you see him, say to him, 'Your punishment of imprisonment, chains and solitary confinement serve as a grossly unequal recompense towards *Jābir 'Atharāt Al-Kirām*!' "

The slave conveyed the message accordingly. Khuzaimah was shocked to learn that *Jābir 'Atharāt Al-Kirām* was his prisoner and immediately had a conveyance prepared for him to proceed to the prison. He took along a number of his officials and entered the prison, where they found 'Ikramah in extremely poor health. When he saw them, he bowed his head down in shame. Khuzaimah slowly stepped forward, lowered himself and kissed 'Ikramah on the forehead.

'Ikramah slowly raised his head and asked, "What has brought you here?"

Khuzaimah replied, "My poor recompense for your kindness."

'Ikramah answered, "May Allāh forgive us both."

Khuzaimah then ordered that his chains be removed and that they be placed around his very own feet. When 'Ikramah saw this, he asked, "What are you doing?"

Khuzaimah replied, "I want to be afflicted with the same punishment."

But, 'Ikramah vowed that he would never allow that. They left the prison and arrived at the home of Khuzaimah. 'Ikramah intended to leave but Khuzaimah did not allow him, "I need to clean you up. I feel ashamed to send you to your wife in this condition." Khuzaimah then called for warm water and himself assisted 'Ikramah to have a bath. Khuzaimah then left 'Ikramah for a short while during which period he gathered a substantial quantity of wealth. He then proceeded with 'Ikramah to his home and left the wealth with him. He also rendered an apology to 'Ikramah's wife for the difficulties he had inflicted upon him.

He then asked 'Ikramah to accompany him to meet the Khalīf Sulaimān ibn 'Abdul Malik who was at Ramlah. The Khalīf was astonished to see Khuzaimah so soon after his appointment as he had not summoned him. He concluded that something important must have brought him and asked, "Why have you come?"

Khuzaimah explained, "I finally identified *Jābir ʿAtharāt Al-Kirām* and I wanted to introduce him to you as you had displayed great eagerness to see him."

The Khalīf asked, "Who is he?"

Khuzaimah replied, "ʿIkramah Al-Fayāḍ."

ʿIkramah was then allowed to enter and the Khalīf welcomed him warmly. When ʿIkramah was comfortably seated, the Khalīf said to him, "ʿIkramah, it was unfortunate that your kindness led to your downfall." The Khalīf then rewarded ʿIkramah with all that he requested and presented him an additional ten thousand dinārs. He also made him governor of Al-Jazīrah, Armenia and Azarbaijān.

He then said to ʿIkramah, "Khuzaimah's position is in your hands. You may choose to keep him or have him removed from office."

ʿIkramah replied, "Keep him in his existing position."

They both then left and remained as governors in their respective areas for the duration of the Khilāfah of Sulaimān ibn ʿAbdul Malik.[1]

A kind gesture never goes unrewarded.

بسم الله الرحمن الرحيم

Patience Earns Rewards

Shaikh Ibrāhīm Al-Hilālī Al-Ḥalabī رحمة الله عليه was a righteous and eminent scholar of his time. He studied various subjects of Islām at Al-Azhar in Egypt. His days as a student were spent in poverty and he would often remain without food for days at a time. On one occasion, hunger compelled him to leave his room at Al-Azhar and go out to beg for food. While walking, he came across a house, the door of which was open and

1 Thamarātul Awrāq, p93; Min Qaṣaṣil ʿArab, p 32

the pleasant fragrance of a tasty meal emitted therefrom. He entered through the door into the kitchen. No one was in sight. He found a pot of food and, with a spoon, he scooped up a portion therefrom. He raised it to his mouth, but at the last moment he held back, as he realised that he did not have permission to eat it. He immediately left the house and returned to his room at Al-Azhar, still hungry.

But not even an hour had elapsed, when one of his teachers, accompanied by another man, entered his room.

His teacher said to him, "This respectable man came to me seeking a righteous student of knowledge to marry his daughter, and I have chosen you for this purpose. Come along now so that we can proceed to his home where the marriage between you and his daughter can be performed. You can then become a part of their family."

Shaikh Ibrāhīm mustered the courage and rose to his feet in obedience to the command of his teacher. He followed them and soon they entered the very same house he had entered earlier.

After settling down, the father married his daughter to him and a meal was served. Amazingly, it was the very same food he had desired to eat, but chose not to partake therefrom. This time he ate from it, saying to himself, "I abstained from eating it because I did not have permission to do so, and due to this Allāh has now presented it to me with honour and dignity in a condition that I am married."

After completing his studies, he returned to Aleppo with his righteous wife, where she bore him a number of righteous children.[1]

Those who exercise patience and adopt piety taste from the fruits of goodness. Allāh ﷻ says:

وَمَنْ يَتَّقِ اللَّهَ يَجْعَلْ لَهُ مَخْرَجًا وَيَرْزُقْهُ مِنْ حَيْثُ لَا يَحْتَسِبُ

"And whoever has taqwa of Allāh, He will make a way out for him,

1 300 Qissah Wa Qissah Wāqiʿiyyah Mu'ath-tharah, p 53; Iʿlām an-Nubalā Bi Tārīkh Ḥalab Ash-Shahbā

and He will provide for him from sources he never imagined." (Sūrah Al-Ṭalāq, verse 2-3)

بسم الله الرحمن الرحيم

The Spiritual Power of Ḥadīth

One of the children of al-Qaʿnabī narrates: My father was an alcoholic who had friends of evil repute. One day, he invited them and sat down in front of his door, awaiting their arrival. Incidentally, Shuʿbah passed by on his donkey, with a number of people following close behind.

"Who is that?" asked al-Qaʿnabī.

"That is Shuʿbah," he was informed.

"And who is Shuʿbah?" he asked.

"A scholar of Ḥadīth," was the reply.

Al-Qaʿnabī, despite being inappropriately dressed in a pair of red trousers, stood up and approached Shuʿbah, saying, "Narrate to me a Ḥadīth!"

Shuʿbah replied, "I only narrate Ḥadīth to those in the field of Ḥadīth and you are not one of them."

Al-Qaʿnabī produced a knife and demanded, "Narrate to me a Ḥadīth or I will hurt you."

Shuʿbah replied, "Manṣūr reported to us from Rabʿī from Abū Masʿūd, who said that Nabī ﷺ said,

اذا لم تستحي فاصنع ما شئت

"If you have no shame, then do as you please."

Al-Qaʿnabī threw the knife to the ground and returned home. He took all the wine bottles he had in his possession and emptied them onto the floor. He then said to his mother, "When my friends arrive, allow them to enter and serve them food. When they have completed their meal, tell them what I have done with the wine, so that they may leave."

Al-Qaʿnabī رحمه الله immediately left for Madīnah, where he studied at the feet of Imām Mālik bin Anas رحمه الله. He eventually began to narrate Ḥadīth from the Imām and then returned to Baṣrah.[1]

A single Ḥadīth of Nabī ﷺ has the power of converting an ardent sinner into a righteous scholar.

Wealth Corrupts

Al-Faḍl ibn Rabʿī narrates: Relations were soured between myself and the Khalīf Ma'mūn, and I was forced into hiding to avoid being apprehended. I would move from one place to another to the extent that my very own family and children were oblivious of my whereabouts. When Ma'mūn arrived in Baghdād, I began to fear for my safety more than ever. I took extra precautions to avoid detection. For a while, I took refuge at the home of a cloth merchant whom I knew fairly well. Ma'mūn intensified his search for me, but was unsuccessful in gathering further information concerning me.

One particular day, my name was mentioned to him. He was furious with Isḥāq ibn Ibrāhīm and insisted that no efforts should be spared in tracking me down. Isḥāq immediately summoned his police chiefs and had an announcement made that a reward of ten thousand dirhams, together with an annual salary of three thousand dinārs, would be awarded to the person who led to my arrest. In addition, any person who was found giving refuge to me would be lashed five hundred times, imprisoned for one year and have his property and wealth confiscated. I did not hear the announcement, but my host did and informed me about it.

1 Kitābut Tawwābīn p 229

He explained, "By Allāh, I cannot provide refuge to you any longer. I do not have any guarantee that my family, neighbours and servants will keep their lips sealed. They may easily be tempted by the reward on offer and report you to the authorities. I would then be arrested with you. On the other hand, if the Khalīf forgives you, you may suspect that I was the one who reported you and this would sour our relationship. It would be in our best interests for you to leave immediately."

This came as a shock to me, but I had no choice but to accept his advice. "I will leave when it is dark," I replied.

"But I cannot bear to wait till nightfall. If you are found with me, both of us will be arrested and punished. The weather is quite hot at present. Disguise yourself and leave without further delay," he advised.

"How should I disguise myself?" I asked.

"Take a portion of hair from your beard and cover your head and face therewith. Wear a tight-fitting outfit and leave," he replied.

I agreed to his suggestion and he brought a pair of scissors. I cut off a large portion of my beard and disguised myself. I then left his house just as the time for ʿAṣr Ṣalāh entered. I proceeded along terrified. I reached a bridge which was quite wet and slippery, and hence deserted. As I commenced crossing it, I noticed a policeman on horseback approaching me. I immediately recognised him as I had appointed him to a prominent position in the police force during my term of office.

As he drew closer, he recognised me and exclaimed, "You are wanted by the Khalīf!" He then reached out to apprehend me. I casually pushed him and his horse away from me. He slipped and fell into one of the boats close to the bridge. People who were close-by quickly rushed to his aid, thinking that he had slipped while trying to cross the bridge. This gave me an opportunity to quickly make my way across the bridge. I did not turn back in case they might recognise me. As I continued I noticed a woman standing at the door of her home.

I pleaded, "I fear for my life. Please grant me refuge and safety."

Without any hesitation she replied, "Enter! She indicated to a room in the house and I climbed up the stairs and entered it."

After an hour, there was a knock at the door. She opened it and her husband entered. I peeped through the door of the room I was in and realised that it was the very same policeman I had pushed off the bridge. His head was bandaged due to the wound he had sustained and his clothing was drenched in blood. His wife enquired what had happened and he related the full incident to her.

He explained, "I missed an opportunity to become a rich man!" He continued to curse me. Little did he realise that I was hiding in his very home. His wife consoled him and he finally settled down.

After I performed Maghrib, and it became dark, she climbed up to my room and enquired from me, "Are you not the same person who escaped from the clutches of my husband?"

"Yes, I am the same person," I replied.

She continued, "You have heard how angry he is with you. Place your trust in Allāh and leave."

I prayed for her. She then descended, gently opened the door so as not to alert her husband and told me to descend. The staircase led into a corridor with a gate at the end. When I reached the gate, I discovered that the guards had locked it. I stood there undecided. After a while, I noticed a man with a Roman key opening the door. I thought to myself, "He appears to me like a Roman, who would surely assist me."

I approached him and asked, "Please grant me refuge and may Allāh do the same for you."

He asked me to enter and I complied. He turned out to be a poor bachelor living by himself. I spent the night at his home. The next day, he left early, but returned at around noon. With him were two porters. One of them was carrying a mat, a pillow, a clay jug, some new plates and a new pot. The other was carrying some bread, fruit, meat and ice. They left all of this with me and closed the door as they departed. I pursued them and quietly enquired from my host why he had gone out of his way to accommodate me.

He answered, "I am a hairdresser and thought that you would dislike eating with me. I, therefore, bought these utensils so that you may prepare food for both of us. I will also bring to you one of my own plates so that you may serve food for me therein. I thanked him for his kindness and stayed with him for three days. I then felt that I was abusing his generosity and said to him, "Brother, you are only obliged to serve a guest for three days. You have fulfilled your responsibility in a gracious and admirable manner, but now I have to leave you."

He replied, "Please do not go and leave me alone. Nobody ever comes to visit me. If you remain here, nobody will ever know your whereabouts. Remain here until Allāh opens your way. You are not a burden to me in any way."

But I refused his offer and set out once again fearing arrest. I proceeded to the house of an old woman whom I knew in my neighbourhood and knocked at her door. She opened it and burst into tears upon seeing me. She praised Allāh for seeing me safe and sound and asked me to enter.

Later that night, while I lay asleep, she quietly slipped out of the house and alerted the police. Isḥāq ibn Ibrāhīm personally arrived with a group of police, who surrounded the house. They took me by surprise and arrested me. I was immediately led before Ma'mūn, barefooted and trembling.

When he saw me, he prostrated for a long time. After raising his head he remarked, "O Faḍl, do you know why I prostrated?"

I replied, "Yes. In gratitude to Allāh, for enabling you to capture your enemy."

He continued, "Not at all! I expressed my gratitude to Allāh for granting me the ability to forgive you. Please relate to me all that has happened to you." .

After hearing my story, he ordered that the old lady be brought to him. She had been anxiously waiting for her reward. When she arrived he asked her, "Why did you have him arrested, despite the gifts he and his family showered upon you?"

She replied, "I was desirous of the reward."

He asked, "Do you have a husband, son or brother?"

She replied that she did not and he ordered that she be given a hundred lashes and imprisoned for life. Ma'mūn then called for the policeman, his wife and the hairdresser. They were all brought and I testified that they were the very same people I had encountered.

He then questioned the policeman, "Why did you make an attempt to arrest him?"

He replied, "I wanted the money on offer as a reward. I knew that he had appointed me to my position in the police, but the quick money blinded me."

Ma'mūn said, "You deserve to be a cupper, who sucks out people's blood, rather than one of my close police officers." He was then left in the care of those who would ensure that he carried out his new duties diligently. Ma'mūn also ordered that his wife be appointed as his household manager, saying, "This is a wise and respectable woman."

The house and furniture of the policeman were given to the hairdresser, who was appointed in place of the former. I was set free and returned home in ease and comfort.[1]

Man has the potential of growth and stagnation. Those who are spiritually trained possess angelic qualities, while those who are not, easily fall prey to the temptations of materialism and worldly riches.

Jannah Purchased for One Dirham

Imām Abū Dāwūd رحمة الله عليه, the renowned muḥaddith and compiler of the Sunan Abū Dāwūd, was on board a ship when he heard a person on the shore sneeze and say, '*Alḥamdulillāh*' (All praise belongs to Allāh). He hired a small boat for one dirham and went ashore in order to reply to the person with the prescribed prayer, '*Yarḥamukallāh*' (May Allāh have mercy upon you).

When he returned to the ship, Imām Abū Dāwūd رحمة الله عليه was asked why he had done so, he answered, "It is possible that the person who sneezed was a *Mustajābut Da'wāt* (one whose du'ās are readily accepted by Allāh).

1 Al-Faraj Ba'dash Shiddah, vol 1, p356

When the people on board later went to sleep, they heard a voice proclaiming, "O people of the ship, Abū Dāwūd purchased Jannah from Allāh at the cost of one dirham."[1]

The righteous servants of Allāh ﷻ go to incredible lengths to earn divine rewards.

Wisdom

A quick-witted reply

A Jew once said to ʿAlī ﷺ: "You people had not yet buried your prophet when the Ansār proclaimed, 'There has to be one leader from amongst us and one from amongst you.' "

ʿAlī ﷺ replied, "The feet of your people had not even dried after emerging from the sea when they said, 'O Mūsā, make for us a deity like their deity.' "[2]

A michief-maker is silenced

Qādhi Abū Bakr ibn Aṭ-Ṭayyib رحمه الله was sent by the Muslims to the Christian king in Constantinople. The Christians respected him and held him in high esteem. As they feared that he would not bow down to the king upon entering the court, they arranged his entry through a small door so that he would be forced to lower his head and bow while entering through it. But, the judge was wise enough to understand their plot and entered while facing his back to the door. Their plan culminated in failure.

1 Fatḥul Bārī, vol 10, p610

2 Thamarātul Awrāq, p67

After taking his seat, one of the Christians mischievously raised the issue of the false accusation made against ʿĀ'ishah رضي الله عنها, "What is the story that is narrated about ʿĀ'ishah, the wife of your Prophet?"

The judge answered, "Two women were falsely accused of adultery: Maryam and ʿĀ'ishah. As for Maryam, she appeared carrying a child while having no husband, while ʿĀ'ishah did not have a child, but had a husband."

His explanation pointed to the fact that the innocence of ʿĀ'ishah رضي الله عنها is a lot clearer and easier to prove than that of Maryam. The Christians were completely dumbfounded with the reply.[1]

Ingenious explanation

A Jew once remarked, "How foolish are the Muslims! They claim that the inhabitants of Jannah will consume food but will not defecate."

Iyās ibn Muʿāwiyah رحمة الله عليه heard the remark and asked him, "Do you defecate all that you consume?"

The Jew replied, "No, Allāh has made a portion of it to serve as beneficial nutrients for the body."

Iyās رحمة الله عليه then explained, "Then why do you deny that Allāh has the ability to make all of it into beneficial nutrients for the inhabitants of Jannah?"[2]

A man of knowledge and wisdom often defeats his adversaries by means of their own logic.

1 Minhāj as-Sunnah An-Nabawiyyah, vol 2, p 56

2 Wafayātul Aaʿyān, vol 1, p 248

A Criminal's Advice to Imām Aḥmad ibn Ḥanbal رحمة الله عليه

ʿAbdullāh ibn Aḥmad ibn Ḥanbal رحمة الله عليه narrates: I would frequently hear my father beseeching Allāh's mercy and forgiveness for Abul Haitham. One day, I asked, "Father, who is Abul Haitham?"

He replied, "When I was led out for lashing and my hands were stretched out, I felt somebody tugging at my clothing. I turned around and saw a young man who asked me, "Do you recognise me?"

I replied that I did not and he continued, "I am Abul Haitham, the notorious scoundrel and criminal, whose name appears in the criminal records of the state. I have been lashed a total of eighteen thousand times, on various occasions. I have endured these lashes with patience in obedience to Shaiṭān and for the sake of this fleeting world. You should bear your lashes with patience as you are in the obedience of Raḥmān and are being punished for the sake of Islām." I was then given eighteen lashes compared to his eighteen thousand. Thereafter a servant of the Amīrul Mu'minīn emerged, saying that I had been forgiven."[1]

Honoured are those souls who bear the punishment of tyrants in defence of the truth.

Honesty

Muḥammad ibn Isḥāq ibn ʿAbdun Najār narrates: A man from our neighbourhood saw a blind man walking by and handed him a purse

1 Ṣifatuṣ Ṣafwah, p 436

of money as Ṣadaqah. It so happened that he had two purses on him, one containing dinārs (gold coins) and the other, dirhams (silver coins). He intended to hand over the dirhams, but mistakenly handed over the dinārs. The blind man took the purse and continued on his way assuming that the purse contained dirhams.

The next morning, he proceeded to the greengrocer and said, "Take this bag of dirhams and count out the amount I am owing you. The remainder you may hand over to me."

When the greengrocer opened the purse he asked in surprise, "Where did you get this purse from?"

The blind man replied, "A man handed it over to me last night."

The greengrocer explained, "The purse contains dinārs. Please take it back."

The blind man took it and returned to the man who had given it to him. He said, "You gave me this as Ṣadaqah. I think that your intention was to give me dirhams, but you made an error. I do not regard this as permissible for me to accept. Please take it back."

The man said to him, "I gave it to you and the matter has been decided. Please come to me at the beginning of every month and I will reward you with something in return for your honesty."

Accordingly, the man would give him five dirhams every month.

Muḥammad ibn Isḥāq ibn ʿAbdun Najār added, "Both the blind man and greengrocer displayed an amazing degree of honesty rarely found amongst men."[1]

Honesty of this nature is rare but a distinguishing trait of the righteous.

1 Rawā'i-ul Qisas, p35; Nishwārul Muḥāḍarah

Qur'ān Memorised in One Month

Moulānā Qāsim Nānotwī set out to perform Ḥaj with a group of Ḥujjāj. During the course of their journey by ship, the crescent was sighted, signalling the beginning of the month of Ramaḍān. Many of his fellow Ḥujjāj were desirous of listening to the entire Qur'ān in Tarāwīh Ṣalāh, but not a single Ḥāfiẓ was on board to accomplish the task. Moulānā too was not a Ḥāfiẓ at the time. After much deliberation, Moulānā agreed to perform the Tarāwīḥ. He would memorise one juz of Qur'ān during the day and recite it in Tarāwīḥ at night. In this way, he memorised the entire Qur'ān in one month.[1]

Memorising the Qur'ān is no simple feat. Fortunate are those who succeed.

Failed the Test

Yūsuf ibn al-Ḥasan says : I came to know that Dhunnūn Miṣrī was one of those pious men of Allāh who knew the Ismul Aa'ẓam[2] and I decided to travel to Egypt to learn it from him. I remained in his company serving him for one year, and then requested, "May Allāh have mercy upon you! I have served you for one year and feel that you are obligated to recompense me for my services. I request that you teach me the Ismul

1 Jawāhir Pāre, vol 1, p 81; Sawāniḥ Qāsimī

2 The greatest name of Allāh through which Allāh fulfils people's needs.

Aaʿẓam. I do not think that you will find anybody worthier of learning it than me."

He remained silent and did not reply to my request for a further six months. One day, he indicated that he would teach it to me. He entered his home and brought to me a dish which was sealed with a cloth on the top. He asked whether I knew a friend of his who resided in Fusṭāṭ. I replied in the affirmative and he requested that I take the dish to him. I left Giza with the sealed dish in my hands.

As I proceeded I thought to myself, "I wonder what the great Dhunnūn Miṣrī is sending as a gift to his friend?" I could not contain my curiosity and unfastened the cover of the dish. The moment I did so a mouse jumped out and escaped. I felt humiliated and angrily said to myself, "Dhunnūn Miṣrī dares to mock at a person like me!"

I returned, burning with rage. The moment he saw me, he realised what had happened and said, "O foolish man, I entrusted you with a mouse and you deceived me. How can I ever trust you with the Ismul Aaʿẓam?" With these words he asked me to leave.[1]

As certain forms of knowledge have the potential of resulting in harm if used incorrectly, the sages are careful who they entrust them to.

بسم الله الرحمن الرحيم

Wisdom of Imām Abū Ḥanīfah رحمة الله عليه

Understanding the temperament of a woman

Once, a heated argument took place between Imām Abū Yūsuf رحمة الله عليه and his wife and she decided to isolate herself from him.

In anger, he said to her, "If you do not speak to me by tonight, you are

1 Thamarātul Awrāq, p 65

divorced." He continued trying every possible means to get her to speak to him, but she adamantly refused to utter a single word.

In desperation, he decided to proceed to Imām Abū Ḥanīfah ﵀ that very night and explain what had transpired. Imām Abū Ḥanīfah ﵀ dressed him up in a new set of clothing, applied scent to his body and placed a splendid Taylasānī shawl around his shoulders with the advice, "Now, proceed to your home and act as if you have no need to speak to her."

Imām Abū Yūsuf ﵀ did as he was advised. When she noticed his attitude she remarked, "It appears as if you have been to the home of a shameless woman!"

Imām Abū Yūsuf ﵀ was overjoyed at her words, by virtue of which their marriage remained intact.[1]

A verdict of honour

Once, a dispute arose between Khalīf Jaʿfar al-Manṣūr and his wife Ḥarrah, who accused him of having no inclination towards her. She requested for the arbitration of Imām Abū Ḥanīfah ﵀ in order to resolve the problem. The Khalīf called for the Imām, and Ḥarrah sat behind a veil to hear the Imām's verdict.

When he arrived the Khalīf asked, "How many wives is a man permitted to have at any one time?"

Imām Abū Ḥanīfah ﵀ replied, "Four."

"And how many bondswomen?" he continued.

Imām Abū Ḥanīfah ﵀ replied, "As many as he desires."

The Khalīf asked, "Can anybody justifiably hold another opinion to this, Islāmically?"

"No," replied Imām Abū Ḥanīfah ﵀.

The Khalīf then addressed his wife, saying, "Ḥarrah, have you heard the verdict?"

At that point, Imām Abū Ḥanīfah ﵀ exclaimed, "This ruling applies to a man who deals justly and fairly with all his wives. As for such a man who is not impartial or fears injustice in dealing with his wives, he should marry only one wife. Allāh ﷻ declares :

1 ʿUqūdul Jumān, p280

فإن خفتم ألا تعدلوا فواحدة

'If you fear that you will not be just then have only one (wife).' (Sūrah Nisā, verse 3)

It is only appropriate that we accept the advice of Allāh and discipline ourselves accordingly," Imām Abū Ḥanīfah ﷺ concluded.

When the Khalīf heard this, he was silent and did not utter a word for a long time. Imām Abū Ḥanīfah ﷺ stood up and left the gathering. When he reached home, he found a servant of the Khalīph's wife at his door, who presented him a significant quantity of money, clothing, a conveyance and a bondswoman as a gift from her side.

Imām Abū Ḥanīfah ﷺ refused to accept the gifts and returned them, saying, "Convey my greetings to her and say to her that I upheld the truth for the pleasure of Allāh. I did not desire the favour of anybody in doing so, nor was I desirous of any worldly reward."

Imām Abū Ḥanīfah ﷺ, far from touching the gifts before him, did not even look at them.[1]

A thief is apprehended

A peacock was stolen from Imām Abū Ḥanīfah's ﷺ neighbourhood. The owner came and complained to him.

Imām Abū Ḥanīfah ﷺ advised, "Remain silent about the matter and do not discuss it further with anybody." The next morning, Imām Abū Ḥanīfah ﷺ went to the Masjid and announced, "Is that person not ashamed who steals a peacock from my neighbour and then arrives to perform Ṣalāh, while the feathers are still visible on his body?"

The man who had stolen the peacock heard the announcement and began to rub his hand over his head.

Imām Abū Ḥanīfah ﷺ noticed him and said, "Please return the peacock!" The man realised that he had been caught out and promptly returned it to the owner.[2]

1 'Uqūdul Jumān, p298; Tabaqātul Ḥanafiyyah; Imām Abū Ḥanīfah, p274

2 'Uqūdul Jumān, p275; Imām Abū Ḥanīfah, p 246

A brilliant stratagem

Al-Aaʿmash was not on favourable terms with Imām Abū Ḥanīfah رحمه الله. One day, he issued a conditional divorce to his wife with the words : "If you inform me that the flour in our home has been depleted, by a verbal declaration, writing a message to me, conveying a message via a third person or making any such indication, then you are divorced from me."

His wife was stunned and sought a solution to save her marriage. People advised her to request Imām Abū Ḥanīfah رحمه الله for an answer. She proceeded and explained to him what had happened.

He explained, "The solution is simple. Tie the empty bag of flour to his trousers or any other portion of his clothing which is convenient for you when he goes to bed at night. When he wakes up from his bed, he will realise that the bag of flour is empty."

She did as he had advised. When Al-Aaʿmash awoke, he realised that his trousers were tied to the empty bag of flour.

He was obliged to submit, "By Allāh, this is surely a stratagem of Abū Ḥanīfah! How can we ever be successful in our plots while he is amongst us? He humiliates us before our wives by exposing our weaknesses to them."[1]

Hidden wealth recovered

A man came to Imām Abū Ḥanīfah رحمه الله and explained, "I buried some wealth in my home, but I have forgotten the exact spot."

Imām Abū Ḥanīfah رحمه الله said to him, "If you have forgotten, it is more unlikely that I should know where it is."

The man was visibly distraught and Imām Abū Ḥanīfah رحمه الله requested a few of his students to join him as they proceeded to the man's home. When they arrived, the Imām asked the man, "In which room do you keep your important household goods?"

The man led them to a room where the Imām asked his students, "If this room belonged to you and you intended hiding something, where would you bury it?"

Each of the students pointed out an area which they considered a good hiding place. From the five different spots they had pinpointed, the

1 ʿUqūdul Jumān, p275; Imām Abū Ḥanīfah, p 247

wealth was found at the third spot which they began to unearth.

Imām Abū Ḥanīfah رحمة الله عليه advised the man, "Be thankful to Allāh Who returned your wealth to you."[1]

Truth is established

A man travelled with his wife to Kūfah. She was exceedingly beautiful, and a resident of Kūfah was taken aback by her beauty and claimed that she was his wife. She mischievously agreed to his false claim. Her rightful husband was disturbed, but could do nothing to prove the validity of his marriage to her. Eventually, the matter was brought to Imām Abū Ḥanīfah رحمة الله عليه.

Together with a number of 'Ulamā' such as Qādhī Ibn Abī Laylā رحمة الله عليه, Imām Abū Ḥanīfah رحمة الله عليه proceeded to the husband's home. At the same time, he ordered a number of other women to also arrive at the home. When seeing each one of the women the husband's dog began to bark. He then requested the man's wife to proceed to the house. When the dog saw her, it began to wag its tail and walk around her happily.

The Imām then said, "The truth has been established." The woman was caught out and acknowledged that she was indeed his wife.[2]

An atheist is silenced

An atheist once approached Khalīf Hārūn Ar-Rashīd and said, "O Amīrul Mu'minīn, scholars of your age such as Abū Ḥanīfah and others have reached consensus that the world has been created by a divine being. Please invite one of your leading scholars to debate this matter with me as I do not believe that the world has been created by a divine being."

Hārūn Ar-Rashīd immediately sent a message to Imām Abū Ḥanīfah رحمة الله عليه, "O Imām of the Muslims, be informed that an atheist has arrived in my court. He denies that the world has been created by a divine being, and wants to debate the matter with you."

Imām Abū Ḥanīfah رحمة الله عليه replied that he would arrive after the Ẓuhr Ṣalāh. At the appointed time, the Khalīf, his courtiers and the atheist waited while the Imām arrived a few minutes late.

---

1 'Uqūdul Jumān, p 267; Imām Abū Ḥanīfah, p236

2 A'immah Arbaa'h Ke Dilchasp Wāqi'āt, p124; Al-Khairātul Ḥisān

After greeting, the Imām was seated, and the atheist asked, "Abū Ḥanīfah, why did you arrive late?"

Imām Abū Ḥanīfah رحمة الله عليه replied, "An amazing incident delayed me. My home is on the other side of the Tigris River. When I arrived at the bank of the river, I noticed an old boat, which had been broken in pieces. As my gaze fell on the scattered pieces of wood they began to move by themselves. Each piece attached itself to the others and soon the boat was formed. All this happened without the aid of a builder. I boarded the boat, crossed the river and arrived here."

The atheist remarked, "Courtiers, have you ever heard such a lie as the one just told to us by your Imām and great leader? This is completely false."

Imām Abū Ḥanīfah رحمة الله عليه then explained, "Do you think that I am speaking lies?"

The atheist replied, "Definitely! Never was a boat ever constructed without the skills of a builder."

Imām Abū Ḥanīfah رحمة الله عليه continued, "Now, listen! If a boat cannot be built without a builder, how is it possible that the universe came into existence without a Creator?"[1]

Knowledge crowned with piety and wisdom goes a long way in establishing the truth and destroying falsehood.

بسم الله الرحمن الرحيم

A Mother's Legacy

One of the governors of Egypt sent for Ibn Al-Furāt رحمة الله عليه and said to him, "I have been harbouring evil intentions regarding you for a long time

1 A'immah-e-Arbaaʿh Ke Dilchasp Wāqiʿāt, p139

now. I would have loved to arrest you and confiscate all your possessions, but I have seen you in my dreams on numerous occasions, resisting and opposing me by means of a loaf of bread. I always see you escaping from my clutches. I then command my soldiers to apprehend you, but when they shoot arrows at you, you defend yourself by means of the loaf of bread in your hand. It appears as though I will never be able to harm you. Please tell me what is the story behind this loaf of bread."

Ibn Al-Furāt رحمة الله عليه replied, "O Governor, since I was a child, my mother would place a loaf of bread beneath my pillow every night. The next morning, she would give it away in Ṣadaqah on my behalf. This remained her practice until her demise. I have continued with this practice ever since. Every night, I place a loaf of bread beneath my pillow and give it out in Ṣadaqah the next morning."

The governor was taken aback and replied, "I will never attempt to harm you from now onwards. In fact, I now entertain good thoughts about you and have developed true love for you."[1]

Parents' habits rub off onto their offspring. Wise are those whose legacy is good actions.

~

Ṣadaqah repels evil.

بسم الله الرحمن الرحيم

A Sage Recalls his Upbringing

Sahl ibn ʿAbdullāh Al-Tustarī رحمة الله عليه was a saint of the highest order. In abstinence and righteous deeds he was without an equal. He grew up in the company of his uncle, Muḥammad ibn Sawwār رحمة الله عليه, who planted the

1 Al Bidāyah Wan Nihāyah, vol 15, p16

seeds of tawḥīd[1] in his heart from an early age.

He narrates: One day, my uncle said to me, "Why don't you remember Allāh Who created you?"

I asked, "How should I remember Him?"

He answered, "Before you sleep every night, say the following three times in your heart, without moving your tongue: Allāh is with me. Allāh is watching me. Allāh is present with me." I followed his advice for some time and then reported back to him. He then advised me to repeat the phrases seven times every night. I again did so and informed him. He then advised me to increase it to eleven. I continued with this practice until the sweetness of it entered my heart.

After a year had passed, my uncle said to me, "Remember what I have taught you and continue with it as long as you live. It will benefit you in this world and the Hereafter." I continued with this and felt the sweetness of it entering me from within.

One day, my uncle addressed me again, "Sahl, a person who realises that Allāh is watching him all the time, would find it difficult to disobey Him? Beware of disobeying Allāh!"[2]

The seeds of Allāh's ﷻ greatness need to be planted when the soil of life is most fertile.

Bearing the Burden of Others

A pious man was burdened with a particularly foul-mouthed wife who caused him a great deal of hardship. Her conduct was so wretched that many in the community came to know about her evil manners.

1 The Oneness of Allāh.

2 Wafayātul Aaʿyān, vol 2, p 429; Ar-Risālutul Qushairiyah

Eventually, some of them decided to advise the pious man, "Why do you tolerate such a woman? She needs to be given a divorce."

He explained, "I know that I have the choice of divorcing her. However, one of two scenarios could occur if I divorce her. If another man does not marry her, she will be in a difficult situation, and if she does remarry, another man will be compelled to endure her evil. For this reason, I am happy to continue living with her evil ways and be a means of protection for others. Why should others suffer if I can prevent it?"[1]

The quality of saving others from harm is a noble trait worthy of emulation.

Zakāt Protects the Wealth of an Englishman

During the days of British rule in India, a number of Englishmen had their residences in an area in the district of Sahāranpur. Their businesses were in the area nearby and many Muslims were employed by them. The English owners would usually reside in the major cities like Delhi, Calcutta, etc. Occasionally, they would visit their businesses to ensure that all was well.

On one occasion, a fire broke out in the residential district, destroying many homes. One of the Muslim workers quickly ran off to Delhi to inform his employer of the calamity. He explained what had transpired. The Englishman was in the process of writing and displayed no concern at all. The worker then raised his voice and explained that all the homes had been raised to the ground. The Englishman was still unconcerned and casually responded that his house would not have burnt down. He

1 Jawāhir Pāre, vol 1, p 31; Hazrat Thānwi Ke Pasandīdah Wāqiʿāt, p110

then continued writing. On the third occasion the employee screamed, “All the homes have been devastated.”

The Englishman replied, “I discharge Zakāt according to the teachings of Islām. Therefore, my possessions will never be afflicted by any harm.”

The employee returned, having fulfilled his responsibility of warning his employer. On arrival, he noticed that all the houses had burnt down except the house of his employer.”[1]

The discharging of Zakāt not only draws divine rewards but protects ones possessions from harm. Even non-Muslims who act in accordance with the teachings of Islām derive worldly benefit therefrom.

بسم الله الرحمن الرحيم

Honesty Converts Highway Robbers

Moulānā Muzaffar Ḥusain Kāndhalwī رحمة الله عليه was a scholar of outstanding virtue and integrity. One day, he set out on a journey from Kāndhla to Gangoh with a number of family members. It was during a time when such journeys were undertaken on foot and by ox-wagons. Roads were dangerous, with highway robbers always on the look-out for easy targets. Soon after commencing their journey, they were surrounded by a gang of robbers. Moulānā instantly realised that the gang was experienced and their intent was to attack and loot the caravan. He quickly jumped down from his ox-wagon and confronted the leader of the gang : “Before commencing with your attack, I plead with you to listen to my request.”

The leader exclaimed, “Make your request!”

Moulānā continued, “I would like to make an agreement with you.”

The leader asked Moulānā what he meant and Moulānā continued,

1 Jawāhir Pāre, vol 3 p156; Āp Beti English, Vol 6, p 89

"We request that you do not harass or lay your hands upon our womenfolk. In return we shall hand over to you all our money, jewellery and valuable possessions."

The leader accepted the proposal and the gang remained stationed where they were. Moulānā returned to the caravan and announced to the females, "Hand over all your jewellery and valuables." The women and children co-operated and Moulānā ensured that nothing remained behind. Once all of it had been gathered he wrapped it in a cloth and handed it over to the gang-leader, saying, "Look! I have brought everything."

The robbers were pleased with their loot and the Moulānā's caravan proceeded. Shortly after departing, Moulānā sensed some sort of excitement and noise amongst the women. Upon enquiry he was told that it was nothing. Moulānā persisted and they finally admitted that a woman amongst them had disclosed that her very precious necklace was still in her possession as she had concealed it beneath her clothing. When Moulānā heard this he immediately instructed that the caravan should proceed no further. He dismounted from his conveyance, walked across to the particular woman and said to her, "Sister, this is a breach of our agreement. We promised the thieves that we would hand over all our valuables to them. Therefore, this necklace belongs to them and not to you. Please hand it over to me so that I could return and hand it over to them." She removed the necklace and handed it over to Moulānā.

Moulānā returned in search of the robbers and found them resting. When they noticed him approaching they assumed that Moulānā had returned with a group in order to attack them. They began gathering their weapons to resist but Moulānā casually replied, "I have not come to fight. I have come to return a trust which belongs to you and I also need to have a word with you."

Moulānā was taken to the leader and said to him, "Brother, I have come to seek your forgiveness and return a trust of yours. You people remained truthful upon your promise and we did not. Here is some jewellery which a woman from amongst us had hidden from you. Since we had promised to hand over all our valuables, this does not belong to us any longer. I have come to hand it over to you. Accept it and please forgive her mistake."

The leader listened to the Moulānā's words with great interest and remarked, "Are you not Moulānā Muzaffar Ḥusain Kāndhalwī? In these parts, he is famous for his honesty."

Moulānā answered, "Yes, I am Muzaffar Ḥusain Kāndhalwī."

The leader immediately fell at the Moulānā's feet in tears and begged for forgiveness. The entire gang of robbers similarly realised their wrongdoing and begged Allāh to forgive them for the wrong they had perpetrated against so many other people. They all pledged allegiance to Moulānā and returned every single item they had taken from Moulānā's caravan. They also promised to return the wealth of every person they had robbed and apologise to every person they had harmed during their past lives of sin."[1]

Truthfulness transforms hearts.

Honouring the Blessed Name of Muḥammad

King Nāṣiruddīn Maḥmūd رحمة الله عليه had a special attendant whose name was Muḥammad, whom he would always address by this name. One day, the king addressed him as Tājuddīn instead of Muḥammad. The attendant complied with the request of his senior and thereafter returned home, but did not attend the court of the king for a period of three days. Nāṣiruddīn noticed his absence and instructed that Muḥammad be brought before him. When he arrived the king asked him why he had been absent.

He replied, "You always used to call me by my name, Muḥammad, but when you addressed me as Tājuddīn, I assumed that you were displeased with me. Out of fear and anguish I separated myself from you. I have

1 Jawāhir Pāre, vol 2, p 67

passed these last three days in extreme distress and sorrow."

The king explained, "I can assure you that I am not displeased with you. I called out to you as Tājuddīn because I was not in the state of wudhū at the time and did not deem it appropriate to express the blessed name of Muḥammad without wudhū."[1]

The intense love of the righteous for Nabī ﷺ is often manifested in remarkable ways.

بِسْمِ اللهِ الرَّحْمٰنِ الرَّحِيْمِ

A Gift Softens the Heart

Bāyazīd Busṭāmī رحمة الله عليه was the sage of the age. His wisdom in winning over the hearts of men was extraordinary. One night, while returning from the cemetery, he ran into a young man who was playing his lute. In anguish, Bāyazīd رحمة الله عليه immediately recited,

لَا حَوْلَ وَلَا قُوَّةَ إِلَّا بِاللهِ الْعَلِيِّ الْعَظِيمِ

"There is no power or might except from Allāh, the Elevated, the Great."

The young man was intoxicated and did not realise who it was. In his stupor, he lifted his lute and struck the saint upon his head so severely that the lute was shattered. Bāyazīd رحمة الله عليه bore the pain patiently and quietly returned home. The next morning, he summoned one of his disciples and requested him to find out the price of a lute. When he was informed, he wrapped the sum of money equivalent to the value of a lute in a cloth and prepared a plate of sweetmeats. He ordered a disciple to deliver these to

1 Jawāhir Pāre, vol 1, p 136; Tārīkh Farishta, vol 1, p276

the young man and instructed, "Say to the young man that Bāyazīd begs his pardon and asks him to accept this sum of money as compensation for his broken lute. Also request him to eat the sweetmeats to remove the sorrow from his heart regarding the broken lute and the episode of the night before."

When the young man realised what had actually transpired, he was overcome with embarrassment. He came to meet Bāyazīd رحمة الله عليه and apologised profusely. He also made tawbah from his sins and a number of his young friends made tawbah along with him.[1]

Acts of kindness and grace soften the heart.

بسم الله الرحمن الرحيم

The Reward for Abstaining from Ḥarām

A pious student was once studying in Delhi and would sleep in a nearby Masjid. One night, a young woman was on her way to visit some of her relatives, who resided in the area, when a riot broke out. She could not manage to escape the commotion and violence in time and quickly ran into the Masjid in fear of her life. When the student noticed her, he was alarmed and explained that the Masjid was not an appropriate place for her to hide. "People may notice us here and my honour will be tarnished. They will then evict me from the Masjid, to the detriment of my studies," he pleaded.

She explained, "If I leave the safety of this Masjid, I fear that my honour and dignity may be blemished by the rioting mobs out in the streets."

Her explanation silenced him as he realised the gravity of the situation.

1 Tadhkiratul Awliyā, p 99, Jawāhir Pāre, vol 1, p 38

He directed her to a corner of the Masjid, where she could remain seated, and returned to continue with his studies. He was immersed in his books for the duration of the night, but occasionally he would place his finger in the flame of a lamp that he was using as a source of light. The young woman too remained awake and intently watched the young man.

Close to dawn, he said to her, "The rioters have dispersed and the streets appear to be safe. I am prepared to accompany you to ensure that you reach your home safely."

"But," she remarked, "I will not leave this Masjid until you explain to me why you kept placing your finger in the flame throughout the night."

He replied, "That is a private matter and I would request you not to question me further about it."

But the young woman would not give in. When he realised that he could not convince her otherwise, he explained, "Shaiṭān was continuously enticing me to fulfil my desires with you. Hence, I kept placing my finger in the flame to remind myself of the unbearable intensity of the fire of Jahannam. If I could not bear the negligible burns from a worldly flame, how would I ever bear the torment of the fire of Jahannam? I am grateful to Allāh that He saved me from sin through out the night."

The young woman left and reached her home safely. She was from a wealthy family and was soon to be married to a family relative. She immediately declined the offer to marry him and said to her parents, "My desire is to marry the student from the Masjid."

Her parents and family tried their utmost to convince her. Others began harbouring suspicions regarding her. When she heard their remarks she explained what had transpired on that fateful night and concluded, "The student has the fear of Allāh within his heart, and such a man will never harm or inconvenience others. My desire is to marry him."

Eventually, her family consented and the nikāh was performed. The student who had lived in a Masjid now became the owner of his very own home, due to his fear of Allāh.[1]

1 Ādābul Muta'allimīn, p23

Allāh ﷻ handsomely rewards a person who abstains from ḥarām.

بسم الله الرحمن الرحيم

Disclosing the faults of others

A wise man once desired to divorce his wife. When questioned about his reason for doing so he answered, "How can I ever disclose the weakness of my wife to strangers?"

After divorcing her, he was again asked why he had done so. He replied, "How can I disclose the weakness of a woman who is a stranger to me? She is no longer my wife."[1]

Couples should not disclose their private and intimate matters, nor divulge each other's faults, errors and shortcomings to others. This presents a real challenge after a divorce, since partners have a tendency to prove that they were innocent and blameless. In many cases, this leads to mudslinging, lies and a great deal of bickering. Divorced couples and their families should part ways amicably and with dignity, honour and integrity. It takes considerable courage and humility to admit to one's wrongs or to forgive and move on, but this is one of the noble traits of the righteous servants of Allāh ﷻ.

1 Jawāhir Pāre vol 2, 247; Mirqāt

بسم الله الرحمن الرحيم

The Value of Time

Yaḥyā ibn Ma'īn رحمة الله عليه is recognised as a great scholar in the science of Ḥadīth. His knowledge of Ḥadīth was extensive and experts, such as Imām Aḥmad ibn Ḥanbal رحمة الله عليه, would say, "If Yaḥyā doubts the authenticity of a particular Ḥadīth then regard his opinion as authoritative."

An interesting incident is quoted which displays his quest for knowledge and the importance he placed upon time. One day, he set out to acquire a Ḥadīth from Muḥammad ibn Fuḍail رحمة الله عليه. As Muḥammad ibn Fuḍail رحمة الله عليه began to narrate from memory, "Ḥammād ibn Salamah has narrated," Yaḥyā stopped him and enquired, "I would prefer you to narrate this Ḥadīth to me by reciting it from one of your books of Aḥādīth rather than from memory."

It was not that Yaḥyā رحمة الله عليه doubted Fuḍail رحمة الله عليه, who was an eminent scholar in his own right, but his care and caution in narrating only sound Ḥadīth led him to make the request. Fuḍail رحمة الله عليه, without any hesitation, stood up to enter his home and bring the particular book. While doing so, Yaḥyā رحمة الله عليه caught hold of his garment and requested, "Narrate it to me verbally first, as I fear that I may not live to have this opportunity again. Fuḍail رحمة الله عليه then proceeded to narrate the Ḥadīth to him verbally and thereafter fetched the book and recited it to him again."[1]

Every moment of life is precious.

1 Al-Musnad Al-Jām'i; Shamā'il Tirmidhī

بسم الله الرحمن الرحيم

Death in a Treasury

There was once a Jew who had amassed a huge amount of wealth. One day, he decided to take a walk through his treasury and look through his riches. In actual fact, he had a guard whose only responsibility was to guard the treasury, but the Jew wanted to ensure that the guard was not secretly pocketing some of his riches. To ensure that the guard was unaware of his presence in the treasury, he chose an appropriate time and quietly slipped in by unlocking the door with his spare key. When the guard arrived he noticed the door open and locked it with his key from the outside. In the meantime, the owner continued counting and checking through the wealth.

After completion, he returned to the door and found it locked. The treasury was solidly built and all he could do was shout as loud as he could, but unfortunately for him, his voice could not reach the outside. He continued shouting for a long time, but nobody could hear him. His treasury was filled with piles of gold and silver, but these were totally valueless in quenching his thirst or satisfying his hunger. He became weaker and weaker until he finally collapsed and died. His wealth could not be of any assistance to him when he needed it most. Rather, it became the primary cause of his death.[1]

Wealth and riches are worthless in the face of death.

1 Jawāhir Pāre, vol 3, p 213; Islāḥi Khuṭubāt

بِسْمِ اللّٰهِ الرَّحْمٰنِ الرَّحِيْمِ

The Honour of a Muslim

Once a veiled woman presented her case before Judge Mūsā ibn Isḥāq, claiming that her husband owed her five hundred dirhams as maḥr. Her husband, who was also present, vehemently disputed her claim.

The lawyer representing the wife said to the judge, "I have brought along witnesses to prove her claim."

One of the witnesses then requested to view the woman's face to confirm her identity. She was about to do so, when the husband intervened, "Should my wife expose her face before a strange man because of this case? I testify in the presence of the judge that I will pay her five hundred gold dirhams, but cannot bear her exposing her face."

When the woman heard her husband's remark and realised his sense of honour and dignity she declared, "I make the judge my witness that I have written off the debt."

The judge was amazed and said, "This incident should be recorded amongst the narrations of good character."[1]

Just as the husband's self-honour compelled him to guard the honour of his wife by not allowing her face to be exposed before strangers, so too should a Muslim's self-honour lead him to defend Islām and Muslims when the need arises.

1 Shua'bul Īmān of Baihaqī

بسم الله الرحمن الرحيم

Maḥmūd and Ayāz

Many poets and writers in the Urdu and Persian languages, such as Shaikh Saʿdī رحمة الله عليه and Moulānā Rūmī رحمة الله عليه, have narrated incidents regarding Maḥmūd and Ayāz. Maḥmūd was a king who conquered Somnāt. He had a favourite amongst his servants by the name of Aḥmad Ayāz. Ayāz, as he was affectionately known, was a simple poor servant, but he possessed one outstanding quality: absolute obedience to his master. This earned him great honour and respect in the sight of Maḥmūd.

The master or his riches

As often happens, a man who is close to the king is looked upon with contempt and malice by his enemies. Ayāz was no exception. Another servant, desirous of the king's favour, one day remarked, "Why does the king favour Ayāz? He is not as great as he is made out to be."

When the remark reached the king's ears, he was rightfully upset, but decided to be patient until a favourable opportunity presented itself. Soon thereafter, the king was on a journey when the conveyance he was travelling on fell to the ground together with all his valuables. He seized the opportunity and announced to his fellow servants, "From these valuables, whatever you lay your hands upon will be yours." The servants began scrambling and grabbing whatever they could, except Ayāz, who remained at the king's side.

The king asked him, "Ayāz, why did you not leave my side and gather some of the valuables?"

Ayāz wisely replied, "O King, I was in your company. Why should I be so foolish as to leave your company for the riches of the world?"

The reply served as a perfect answer which the king used to silence Ayāz's malicious critics, saying, "This is why Ayāz is a favourite in my sight."

Just as Ayāz wisely preferred the king over his riches, a wise man prefers the love of Allāh ﷻ over worldly riches.

Humble beginnings

When Ayāz first arrived at the court of Maḥmūd, he possessed only a tattered shawl and an old piece of fur. After donning the clothing of the court, he kept his old clothing locked in a room. Everyday, he would enter the room by himself for a few moments and look at his old clothing, while addressing himself, "Ayāz, not long ago you arrived here with these tattered clothes, but today you are closely attached to the king. Never forget your origin. You enjoy the favours of the king in abundance, but don't ever become proud and boastful. Rather be grateful that a person, who once dressed in tattered clothing, has won the favour of a great king and is the envy of all the courtiers and servants."

Slowly but surely the news of Ayāz and his daily seclusion in the room spread. His enemies could not bear to see a simple and poor man like Ayāz enjoying the king's favours. They began discussing the matter, "Why does he seclude himself and what has he got locked up in that room? Perhaps, he is stealing from the treasury and gathering it in there! The king should be alerted about this so that Ayāz's true colours are exposed."

After collectively agreeing to the idea they approached the king and explained, "Beloved King, Ayāz is a thief and a hypocrite. He does not have true love for you. We have proof that he is stealing from your treasury and gathering all the riches in a locked room."

The king did not entertain the slightest doubt in Ayāz's loyalty, but to silence them and prove Ayāz's honesty and sincerity he announced that Ayāz's room would be searched that night. Ayāz's enemies were overjoyed. "Finally, Ayāz shall be disgraced," they thought.

That night, the lock to his room was broken and the investigating team began their search. But, they could find nothing, but a tattered shawl and an old piece of fur. They went to the extent of digging open the floor to check whether he had hidden anything in a secret vault. Finally, exhausted and disappointed, they presented themselves before the king, greatly embarrassed. They had no choice but to apologise for thinking evil of Ayāz.

The incident increased the king's affection for him and he asked, "Ayāz, why did you keep these old clothes locked in the room?"

Ayāz replied, "Beloved King, these clothes serve as a lesson for me. I look at them to remind myself that I am constantly enjoying the king's favours and gifts, but I once possessed nothing but a pair of tattered clothing."

The wise are always humble and simple. They choose gratitude over pride and arrogance.

True love

One day, the king wanted to test his courtiers. He asked for a pearl to be brought from his treasury and placed it in the hands of his finance minister with the question, "How much is this worth?"

The minister replied, "It is extremely valuable. Its value is in excess of two hundred donkey-loads of gold."

Then the king instructed, "I command you to crush it."

The minister refused, saying, "I am your well-wisher and will never allow any harm to come to your treasury."

The king presented a small reward to the minister and then placed the pearl in the hands of another close courtier with the same instruction.

The courtier replied, "This pearl is worth half your kingdom. May Allāh protect it! My hands could never crush such a valuable object. An act of this nature is defiance of your honour."

The king similarly rewarded him with a small gift and praised him. Thereafter, the king made the same request to a total of sixty-five courtiers. Each of them responded in the same manner and received an award and a word of praise. He then called for Ayāz and said, "All the courtiers have estimated the value of this pearl. How much do you think it is worth?"

Ayāz replied, "Dear King, the pearl is far more valuable than any price I attach to it."

"Crush it to pieces!" the king commanded.

Ayāz was a wise man and realised that the king was merely testing him. He immediately crushed it. As he did so, the court erupted with the courtiers' disapproval. They proclaimed, "Only a fool would do such a thing!"

Ayāz replied calmly, "My fellow courtiers! Is the pearl more valuable than the command of the king? You all had your sights focussed upon the pearl instead of the king. I would never divert my gaze from the king to the pearl. This would be a form of defiance because I would be disobeying the command of the king.[1]

Just like Ayāz wisely gave preference to the king's command, so too should one preferentially obey the commands of Allāh ﷻ.

Smiles and Tears

ʿĪsā عليه السلام once met Yaḥyā عليه السلام. ʿĪsā عليه السلام would smile a lot while Yaḥyā عليه السلام would cry a lot.

ʿĪsā عليه السلام asked, "O Yaḥyā, have you lost hope in the mercy of Allāh to such an extent that your crying does not cease?"

Yaḥyā عليه السلام responded by asking, "O ʿĪsā, do you feel so safe from the wrath of Allāh that you smile all the time?"

1 Jawāhir Pāre, vol 2, p 120-126

After a while, an angel appeared to them and said, "Allāh has commanded me to come to you and explain His verdict regarding your respective conditions. O ʿĪsā, remain smiling in public, but in seclusion cry like Yaḥyā. And, O Yaḥyā, in privacy continue shedding tears, but in public smile with others. It should not become such that people see a prophet of Allāh in tears all the time. They would lose hope in His mercy when they see you like this."[1]

The life of man must be a balance between smiles and tears.

بسم الله الرحمن الرحيم

Death on Īmān

Sayyid Aḥmad Shahīd رحمة الله عليه, the great mujāhid, fought many wars in the service of Islām and was finally martyred in the Battle of Bālākot. On one occasion, a Muslim person, commonly known as Rājah, joined his army. However, at the crucial moment when the two armies came face to face, he abandoned the Muslims and joined the army of Sher Singh. A few moments later, a Sikh from the army of Sher Singh left his camp and accepted Islām at the hands of Sayyid Aḥmad Shahīd رحمة الله عليه. He was given the name ʿAbdullāh.

When the battle commenced, Rājah was in the forefront fighting alongside the Sikhs. A bullet struck him and he fell to the ground and died. Soon thereafter, a bullet was fired by the Sikhs and hit the new Muslim, ʿAbdullāh. He too fell to the ground, but his death was one of a Shahīd.[2]

1 Jawāhir Pāre, vol 2, p 168

2 Jawāhir Pāre, vol 2, p20; Sīrat Sayyid Aḥmad Shahīd

The success or failure of an individual cannot be judged with certainty from his life in this world. Instead, a person's final moments serve as the true barometer of success or failure. Fortunate are those who pass away with the kalimah on their tongues. Unfortunate are those who pass away in the condition of disbelief and sin.

Parent's Legacies

ʿUmar Ibn ʿAbdul ʿAzīz رحمة الله عليه passed away leaving behind eleven sons. His estate consisted of only seventeen dinārs. From this, five dinārs were used for his burial shroud, and another two for his grave. The remaining ten dinārs were equally distributed amongst his sons. Each son received a small sum of nineteen dirhams.

Hishām ibn ʿAbdul Malik also passed away leaving behind eleven sons. From his estate, each son received a hefty sum of ten thousand dirhams. Soon thereafter, one of the sons of ʿUmar Ibn ʿAbdul ʿAzīz رحمة الله عليه was seen dispatching a hundred of his horses fully-laden with goods in jihād. In sharp contrast, one of the sons of Hishām was seen begging.

After quoting this incident, ʿAllāmah Damīrī remarked, "This is nothing strange. ʿUmar ibn ʿAbdul ʿAzīz had trained his sons Islāmically and handed them into the care of Allāh, Who made them independent and wealthy. Hishām taught his sons about the world and in return Allāh tested them with poverty."[1]

1 Ḥayātul Ḥayawān vol 2, p204; Jawāhir Pāre, vol 3, p272

Wise men lead their offspring along the path of Islām, while the ignorant teach their offspring to become slaves of the world.

بسم الله الرحمن الرحيم

True Worth of Worldly Empires

Hārūn Ar-Rashīd, the Khalīf of the Muslims, requested the righteous Ibn Simāk رحمة الله عليه for some advice. Ibn Simāk رحمة الله عليه noticed that Hārūn Ar-Rashīd had a glass of water in his hand and asked, "Amīrul Mu'minīn, if you were deprived of the bounty of drinking water, would you be prepared to exchange your entire kingdom for it?"

"Yes, I will certainly be happy to do so," replied the Khalīf.

Ibn Simāk رحمة الله عليه then asked, "If you did not have the ability to urinate, and water collected in your body, would you be prepared to exchange your entire kingdom in return for the bounty of urination?

"Yes, I will be happy to do so," replied the Khalīf.

Ibn Simāk رحمة الله عليه then wisely remarked, "What goodness is there in a kingdom which is not even equal to a glass of water and urine?"

Hārūn Ar-Rashīd realised the truth of the wise man's explanation and was reduced to tears.[1]

Worldly riches and splendour are worthless when compared with the bounty of good health.

1 Jawāhir Pāre, vol 3, p113; Al-Kanzul Madfūn

A Greater Fool

Baḥlūl رحمة الله عليه was a pious man who lived during the Khilāfah of Hārūn Ar-Rashīd. Although people often looked down upon him, Baḥlūl رحمة الله عليه, was no fool. He would often enter the court of the Khalīf and casually discuss matters of mutual interest. One day, he entered the court and found Hārūn Ar-Rashīd with a knife in his hand.

The Khalīf jokingly remarked, "Baḥlūl! I have a request."

"What is it?" asked Baḥlūl رحمة الله عليه.

He replied, "I am handing this knife over to you as a trust. If you find a greater fool than yourself in the entire world then you should hand this knife over to him as a gift from me."

Baḥlūl رحمة الله عليه agreed and the Khalīf handed it over to him. The request was actually intended to mock at Baḥlūl رحمة الله عليه, with the message that nobody was more foolish than him. Baḥlūl رحمة الله عليه made no fuss about the joke and left the court with the knife.

The years passed by. One day, the news reached Baḥlūl رحمة الله عليه that Hārūn Ar-Rashīd was seriously ill and bedridden. Various forms of medication were administered, but without any success. Baḥlūl رحمة الله عليه decided to visit the Khalīf.

As he entered he asked, "Amīrul Mu'minīn, how are you feeling?"

The Khalīf replied, "My time is up. I have commenced my journey."

"Where are you going?" asked Baḥlūl رحمة الله عليه.

The Khalīf answered, "I will soon leave this world for the Hereafter."

Baḥlūl رحمة الله عليه asked, "After how many days will you return?"

The Khalīf replied, "This is the journey of the Hereafter! Nobody returns from this journey."

Baḥlūl رحمة الله عليه asked, "If you will not return, how many armies and delegations have you sent forth to welcome you and make your stay there comfortable?"

The Khalīf replied, "Again you are talking like a fool! A man goes alone on this journey. No companions, bodyguards or armies may accompany him."

Baḥlūl رحمه الله asked in surprise, "I am surprised that you have not prepared for a journey of such long duration and for a destination from which there is no return. I remember well how you used to carefully prepare and send out armies and soldiers ahead of your departure while you were healthy. Why were you so lax regarding this journey?"

The Khalīf answered, "On this journey no army or soldiers are allowed to accompany a person."

Baḥlūl رحمه الله continued, "I have something which you gave me as a trust many years ago: a knife. You asked me to hand it over to a person who was more foolish than myself. I searched for such a person but could not find one, until today. You are more foolish than me. I noticed how you would go out of your way to prepare for the shortest of journeys. Months ahead of time, you would arrange food, tents, bodyguards and so much more. You would send these ahead of your departure so that your entire journey would be in luxury. But, for such a journey from which there is no return, you have prepared nothing! I have not found a more foolish man than you. I would like to return your knife to you."

The Khalīf heard the explanation and burst into tears. He exclaimed, "Baḥlūl! You have spoken the truth. I regarded you as a fool my entire life, but you are a wise man. You understood the reality of life better than me. I have wasted my life in this world by not preparing for my journey towards the Hereafter."[1]

True intelligence lies with those who pursue the greater goal of preparing for the life of the Hereafter.

1 Jawāhir Pāre, vol 3, p 210; Iṣlāḥī Khuṭubāt

A Lofty Rank

One day, Hārūn Ar-Rashīd took the hand of Imām Mālik and they proceeded to the grave of Nabī ﷺ. When they arrived, he asked the scholar, "Inform me about the status of Abū Bakr and ʿUmar in relation to Nabī ﷺ."

Imām Mālik replied, "Their proximity to him while he lived is the same as their proximity to him after his demise."[1]

Truly blessed are the two Ṣaḥābah who lie beside the greatest of creation.

بسم الله الرحمن الرحيم

Remembrance of Death

Curtailing the aspirations of the soul

Mullah ʿAlī Qārī mentions that his spiritual mentor, Moulānā Nūruddīn ʿAlī Muttaqī, would have small lockets made up, upon which the word "death" was engraved. He would then hand these out to his disciples to hang around their necks as a constant reminder that death was hovering over them. This would serve a dual purpose. It would curtail their worldly desires and aspirations, while creating within them a yearning to increase their good deeds.

1 Tartībul Madārik vol 2, p 19; 100 Qissah Wa Qissah Min Hayāt al-Imām Mālik, p 27

A wise king

A righteous king was always conscious of the Hereafter. To remind himself that death was imminent, he had a servant who would stand behind him all the time uttering the word "death" repeatedly.[1]

Reflection upon the temporary nature of this worldly life serves as a spiritual remedy for diseases that afflict the soul.

بسم الله الرحمن الرحيم

Reward for Chastity

The Crusades were a series of wars in which the Christians fought the Muslims with the aim of regaining Musjidul Aqṣā. The heart-rending incident that follows occurred during that critical period of time. Al-Amīr Shujāʿuddīn Muḥammad Ash-Shirāzī, an official of a state in Cairo, narrates: "We once spent a night in the company of a man, who resided in the mountainous regions on the outskirts of the city. He was tremendously generous and hospitable towards us. He was dark in complexion and the signs of old age had caught up with him, while his children were exceedingly fair and beautiful.

We were taken aback and asked, "Are these really your children?"

"Yes," he explained, "I notice that you are surprised at their fair complexion and my dark complexion."

We acknowledged our surprise, and he continued, "My life story is a strange one indeed. The mother of these children is European and I married her while I was a young man, during the days of An-Nāṣir Ṣalāḥuddīn."

"Please narrate your story to us. How did you come to marry her?"

1 Jawāhir Pāre, vol 3, p 143; Mirqāt

we asked.

He commenced, "I was a cotton farmer during my youth. On one occasion, I spent five hundred dinārs in planting trees and harvesting the cotton but could not find a buyer willing to pay more than what I had invested. I tried taking it to other areas of the city, but my efforts proved fruitless. Eventually, I took my goods and proceeded to the city of Acre, where I sold some of it on credit and the remainder I kept in my possession. I rented a shop for a period of time where I continued selling it at my leisure. One day, during the course of business, I noticed a young European woman approaching. Her face and hair were uncovered, as was the habit of all the European women when they walked in the streets. She entered and purchased some cotton. She was exceedingly beautiful. So overwhelmed was I by her beauty, that I dealt graciously with her and sold the cotton to her at a very discounted price. She soon left, but returned a few days later to purchase some more. I concluded the sale with a larger discount than the first time. In this way, she became my regular customer. After some time, she realised that I was attracted to her. One day, I quietly said to the old woman who usually accompanied her, "I am in love with this young woman and would like to spend a night with her. Can you help?"

The old woman mentioned my request to the young woman, who was not keen on the idea.

"But," I persisted, "my heart and soul are infatuated with love for her. I will do anything to be with her." She eventually agreed to my request on condition that I pay her fifty dinars. I counted them out and handed them over to the old woman. They left, saying, "We will meet you later tonight."

I left my shop earlier than normal and proceeded to purchase the best of food, drinks, sweetmeats, candles and other luxuries that I could afford. That evening, the young woman arrived at my home. We ate and drank to our fill late into the night. The time had arrived to fulfil my desires with her. At this critical juncture, I felt embarrassed and asked myself, "Are you not ashamed of Allāh? You are a stranger in these lands and you have the audacity of disobeying Allāh with a strange Christian woman!"

I boldly proclaimed, “O Allāh, I make You my witness that I have decided to abstain from this woman tonight, out of shame for You and because I fear Your punishment.” I then slept till the morning. She did likewise and when the sun rose she left without a word. I awoke and proceeded to my business, where I sat down to ponder. All of a sudden, I noticed the young woman and her elderly companion crossing the road towards my shop. I quickly realised that she was very angry, but she still appeared to me more beautiful than the full moon. I again found myself uncontrollably attracted towards her. I said to myself, “Who do you think you are? You have the opportunity of fulfilling your burning desires with this beautiful woman, yet you resist the impulse!”

I dashed out and caught up with them. I pleaded to the old woman for a second chance, but she was adamant. Finally, she agreed, “I will allow her to come to you again if you pay me a hundred dinars.” I readily agreed to her condition, counted out the money and handed it over to her. That night, she came to me again, but my thoughts of the previous night overpowered me once more. I refrained from fulfilling my desires with her out of shame for Allāh. The next morning, she left and I proceeded to my shop. Again she approached me, but this time she spoke to me like a complete stranger, “From now on, I will not allow you to enjoy my company, except on condition that you pay me five hundred dinars. I do not care if you die of sorrow over me.”

I realised that her asking price was excessive, but I made a firm intention to pay it, even if I had to sell all my cotton in acquiring the amount. As I pondered over my plight, I heard an announcement being made, “O Muslims! The truce that was agreed upon between you and us has ended. You have been given respite until this Friday to settle your affairs and leave our lands.”

I realised that this announcement was the point of separation between me and the woman I loved. I began to collect the monies that were due to me and made agreements for the remainder to be paid up promptly. I left Acre with the cotton I had, but my heart was still drowned in love for the Christian woman I was forced to leave behind.

I reached Damascus and began to sell the cotton. I earned significant profits from the sales because the truce had ended and people were eager to buy the stocks I had. Allāh made me a rich man. I left the cotton trade and began to buy and sell slaves in the hope that my love and desire for the European woman would leave my heart. Three years passed and the political landscape changed considerably. Sulṭān An-Nāṣir captured many lands, including those along the coast after the decisive battle of Ḥiṭṭīn, by the grace of Allāh. Soon thereafter, I was approached by the king's attendants, who explained that the king wanted to purchase a slave-woman from me. I presented a beautiful woman and they agreed to the purchase price of a hundred dirhams. They paid ninety in cash and returned to the king to request for the remaining ten.

There were no more dirhams in the treasury that day and the king instructed, "Escort him to the tent where the captured European female prisoners of war are housed. Allow him to choose one of them in lieu of the ten dirhams owed to him." I proceeded to the tent and immediately recognised the beautiful woman I had known during my days of cotton-trade in Acre. I requested for her and headed home. When we were in seclusion, I sat down with her and asked, "Do you recognise me?"

"No," she answered.

I explained, "I am that cotton-trader who had dealings with you. You had taken money from me a few times and finally said that you would not meet me unless I paid you five hundred dinars. Now, I own you and have paid a mere ten dinars!"

She replied, "Extend your hand. I bear witness that there is no deity worthy of worship besides Allāh and Muḥammad is the messenger of Allāh."

She accepted Islām in my presence and thereafter, proved to be a good Muslim in her conduct and dealings. I still desired to be with her but decided to marry her by performing nikāh according to the proper Islāmic teachings. I proceeded with her to Judge Ibn Shaddād who listened intently to my story and finally performed our nikāh. She was now my wife!"

I continued with the army and we entered Damascus. Soon thereafter, a messenger arrived with orders from the king that all slaves be returned as there had been some sort of agreement between the Muslim and Christian kings. All slaves were returned except my wife. They noticed her absence and began to search for her. They were directed to my home and I realised that her time was up. Sorrowfully, I proceeded with her to the king's court.

With the European messenger at his side, the king instructed her, "Proceed to your homeland and your husband. We have freed you and all the others."

She replied, "Sulṭān, I have accepted Islām as my faith. I am now pregnant as you can see. The Europeans will derive no benefit from me any longer."

The European messenger again asked for clarification from her, "Do you prefer this Muslim husband of yours or your former European husband?" She replied as she had done before.

The Europeans could not insist on her return and I left the court with her. They summoned me again, but this time the European messenger said, "Her mother has entrusted me with something which I need to hand over to your wife. She had said to me: "My daughter has been enslaved and I request you to pass this onto her."

They handed me a box and I returned home. She opened it and found a cloth which her mother had woven for her. There were also two golden containers filled with coins. One contained fifty dinars and the other, a hundred dinars, in the very same condition I had given her all those years ago."

The old man ended his fascinating narrative with the casual remark, "These children you see before you are from her and the food you have consumed was prepared by her."[1]

Abstaining from sin draws immense rewards. Those who choose to tread the path of chastity and purity attain the spiritual bliss that comes with it.

1 Min Qaṣaṣil ʿArab, p 69

Anxiety of an Ant

Shaikh Saʿdī رحمة الله عليه narrates: Shaikh Shiblī رحمة الله عليه once purchased some barley and returned home carrying it on his head in a sealed cloth. After a short while, he opened it and noticed an ant running out. To the Shaikh the ant appeared anxious as it dashed around uneasily.

Shaikh Shiblī رحمة الله عليه was saddened at its pitiful condition and began to ponder, "Where could it have come from? Surely it must be restless and fearful due to separation from its abode."

That night, he spent tossing and turning, unable to sleep. The next morning, he picked up the cloth, fastened it and set out towards the city. After arriving at the shop where he had purchased the barley, he opened the cloth and set the ant free.[1]

The close servants of Allāh سبحانه وتعالى meticulously guard against causing any sort of harm to the creation.

~

In days gone by, men were saddened at the anxiety of an ant. Today, man has sunk into such an abyss of destruction that such heinous crimes as abortion are justified by so-called progressive governments of the world.

بسم الله الرحمن الرحيم

Ingenuity of Imām Abū Ḥanīfah رحمة الله عليه

The forces of evil are notorious for plotting in order to tarnish the

1 Jawāhir Pāre, vol 1, p42; Bustān

reputation of those who tread the path of truth. The hypocrites plotted against Nabī ﷺ by making false accusations against his wife ʿĀ'ishah رضي الله عنها. However, truth always prevails. The evildoers and their lies are bound to fail sooner or later.

Imām Abū Ḥanīfah رحمة الله عليه was one such man of truth whom the evildoers desired to harm. One day, they hatched a sly plot to tarnish the reputation of the Imām so that he would lose his respect amongst people. They bribed a young widow who readily agreed to their nefarious plot. While returning home from the Masjid every night, Imām Abū Ḥanīfah رحمة الله عليه would pass by her home. One night, she appeared before him with her body and face completely concealed and exclaimed in desperation, "Imām! My husband is about to pass away and is intending to make some sort of bequest, but I cannot understand it. Please come quickly!"

Imām Abū Ḥanīfah رحمة الله عليه followed her into her home and, after entering, she quickly locked the door behind him. The Imām's enemies, who had slyly concealed themselves within the home, emerged and began slandering him, "Imām Abū Ḥanīfah, what are you doing in this private residence in the company of a strange young woman at this late hour? You evil man!"

They immediately handed the innocent Imām and the young woman over to the police. The news spread like wildfire and soon reached the ears of the governor, who instructed that both be put behind bars for the duration of the night. The case would be heard the next morning. Accordingly, they were enclosed in a small cell. The Imām was in the state of wudhū and immediately commenced performing Nafl Ṣalāh. The young woman could do nothing but watch the Imām, and soon realised her error of attempting to vilify such a respectable man and waited for the Imām to complete his Ṣalāh. She then begged his forgiveness and confessed to their mischievous plot.

The Imām declared, "We cannot undo what has occurred, but I have a plan that can clear our names."

"What?" she quickly asked.

Imām Abū Ḥanīfah رحمة الله عليه explained, "Plead to the guard outside to let you free so that you can return home for a moment. Convince him that you were brought here without any explanation and that you need to attend to an essential task which cannot be delayed. Ask him to accompany you so that he does not doubt your intention to return. When he agrees you should proceed to my home, where you should enlighten my wife regarding the proceedings. Ask her to disguise herself by donning your clothing and request her to come here immediately."

The young woman succeeded in convincing the guard, and the Imām's wife reached his prison cell in a short while. The next morning, the governor summoned the Imām and his wife. The Imām's enemies were in attendance in large numbers, anxious to see the Imām's reputation tarnished.

When the case was brought forward the governor asked, "Abū Ḥanīfah, you are a great scholar. How could you engage in such a major crime?"

Imām Abū Ḥanīfah رحمة الله عليه asked, "What are you implying?"

The governor continued, "You were caught in the presence of a strange young woman in privacy late at night."

Imām Abū Ḥanīfah رحمة الله عليه explained, "She is no stranger to me."

The governor asked, "Who is she to you?"

Imām Abū Ḥanīfah رحمة الله عليه pointed to his father-in-law and said, "Ask this honourable man to clarify who she is."

The elderly man was called forward and he explained, "This is my daughter. I handed her over in marriage to Imām Abū Ḥanīfah at such and such a place."

The enemies were left utterly defeated by the amazing ingenuity with which Allāh ﷻ had blessed the Imām.[1]

Only fools attempt to tarnish the reputation of the righteous servants of Allāh ﷻ.

1 Allāh Ke Āshiqo Ke Hālāt, vol 2, p782

The Knowledge of Imām Muḥammad رحمة الله عليه

Kitābul Aṣl is a book of jurisprudence which was compiled by Imām Muḥammad Ibn Ḥasan Shaibānī رحمة الله عليه, the famous student of Imām Abū Ḥanīfah رحمة الله عليه. Imām Shāfiʿī رحمة الله عليه memorised it from cover to cover and then wrote his magnum opus, Kitābul Umm.

Imām Shāfiʿī رحمة الله عليه himself mentions, "I spent ten years in the company of Imām Muḥammad and acquired knowledge from him equivalent to that of a camel-load."

A Jewish rabbi, after studying the Kitābul Aṣl of Imām Muḥammad رحمة الله عليه, accepted Islām with the proclamation, "If this is the book of your junior Muḥammad, what is there left to say about the book (Qur'ān) of your senior Muḥammad (i.e. Nabī ﷺ)?"[1]

May Allāh ﷻ be pleased with the tremendous contributions of our erudite scholars and luminaries in the field of fiqh.

بسم الله الرحمن الرحيم

An Ungrateful Man

Wahab ibn Munabbih رحمة الله عليه narrates: Once the angel of death was ascending towards the heavens with the soul of a king whose tyranny was second to none. On his way, he met some angels who asked, "From all the souls of men that you have taken, whose did you feel the most compassion for?"

The angel of death replied, "I was once instructed to take the soul of a woman who had just given birth to a young baby boy. She was alone in

1 Jawāhir Pāre, vol 1, p 247; Bulūghul Amānī

a jungle and I wondered what would happen to the baby who would be left alone without any living being in sight. After taking her soul, I was touched by such compassion which I had never experienced before."

The angels explained, "That same baby grew up to become the tyrant king, whose soul you are now taking up."

The angel of death was astounded and exclaimed, "O Allāh, You are pure, most kind and You do as You please."[1]

How many a person grows up in the shadow of Allāh's ﷻ mercy, only to flagrantly disobey Him without displaying any remorse! How many a person lives off the kindness of others, only to ignore them when he no longer requires their assistance! Truly, man becomes ungrateful when wealth intoxicates his sense of dignity and reason.

بسم الله الرحمن الرحيم

The Loose Brick

ʿUmar Ibn ʿAbdul ʿAzīz رحمة الله عليه had a staircase in his home. The staircase had one particular brick which was loose and would shake whenever he used to step upon it. One day, his servant decided to attach the brick firmly into place. The next time ʿUmar ibn ʿAbdul ʿAzīz رحمة الله عليه used the staircase he immediately realised that the brick was no longer loose and asked, "Why does this brick no longer shake?"

The servant replied, "We decided to repair it by attaching it firmly into place."

ʿUmar ibn ʿAbdul ʿAzīz رحمة الله عليه replied, "The loose brick served as a gentle reminder to me. Whenever I stepped onto it I would remember the Bridge of Ṣirāṭ, and declare, "O Allāh, when I am afraid of a small brick falling

1 Iḥyā ʿUlūmuddīn, vol 15, p 2871; Jawāhir Pāre, vol 1, p 206

from a staircase, how will I be able to cross the Bridge of Ṣirāṭ?"[1]

Such is the insight of the righteous. They understand the deeper meanings of life which are beyond the material pleasures of this world.

بسم الله الرحمن الرحيم

A Mother's Love is Priceless

ʿAllāmah Shihābuddīn Aḥmad Qalyūbī narrates the story of a pious man who observed a person carrying a woman on his shoulders, while performing Ṭawāf of the Kaʿbah. The pious man asked him who the woman was.

He replied, "This is my mother. I have been carrying her like this on my shoulders for the past seven years. Have I fulfilled her rights?"

The pious man answered, "Never! Never! If you carried her on your shoulders for a thousand years, it would not be equal to one night in which she held you in her arms and gave you milk to drink."

When the man heard the answer he was reduced to tears.[2]

A mother's love and favours are priceless.

1 Jawāhir Pāre, vol 1, p 169

2 Jawāhir Pāre, vol 1, p 155

The Sacrifice of Life

Moulānā Maḥmūd Ḥasan رحمة الله عليه was one of those ʿUlamā' who gave his life fighting the oppressive British rule in India. The British were in conspiracy with Sharīf Ḥusain, who treacherously broke away from the ʿUthmānī Khilāfah and established his own regime. On the instruction of the British, a messenger was sent with a letter to Moulānā Maḥmūd Ḥasan رحمة الله عليه, who was in Makkah at the time, requesting Molānā's signature. The letter was supposedly from the side of the ʿUlamā' who taught in the precincts of the Ḥaram and proclaimed that all the Turks were disbelievers because they had ousted Sulṭān ʿAbdul Ḥamīd Khān. The letter also declared the break-away of Sharīf Ḥusain to be in order. The ʿUthmāni Khilāfah in Turkey was declared null and void.

Moulānā Maḥmūd Ḥasan رحمة الله عليه refused to sign the letter, saying, "I do not teach in the Ḥaram and further, I hail from India and not from the blessed lands."

The messenger left without a word, but a number of Moulānā's close associates warned him that the repercussions of his refusal could be disastrous.

Moulānā boldly explained, "The content of the letter contradicts the teachings of Islām."

A few days later, Sharīf Ḥusain ordered the capture and imprisonment of Moulānā Maḥmūd Ḥasan رحمة الله عليه together with a number of his companions. Moulānā spent approximately three and a half years as a prisoner in Malta. Following his release, Moulānā returned to Deoband where he continued his opposition to the British with even greater zeal. However, within a short period of time, Moulānā left this temporary sojourn for the eternal life of the Hereafter. [1]

1 Jawāhir Pāre, vol 2, p315

May Allāh ﷻ bless our pious predecessors for their resilience and courage in opposing the oppressors and upholding the truth.

Complaining is Counterproductive

Luqmān ﷺ was a prophet according to some scholars, while others maintain that he was not. However, according to all, he was blessed with wonderful insight and wisdom. At one stage of his life, he was employed as a labourer in an orchard.

One day, the owner entered the orchard and requested for some fruit, which was brought to him. He sliced it and gave a piece to Luqmān ﷺ, who began to eat it with great relish. Seeing this, the master assumed that it was probably very tasty. He placed a piece into his mouth, but immediately spat it out as it proved to be extremely bitter.

Astonished and irritated, he asked, "Luqmān, this fruit is extremely bitter. How do you eat it with such great pleasure?"

Luqmān ﷺ replied, "Yes, I have realised that it is very bitter."

The master continued, "But, why did you not say so earlier?"

Luqmān ﷺ replied, "How can I make such a statement! When I have eaten sweet fruit thousands of times from the hand that provides me, why should I complain for one piece of bitter fruit?"[1]

Never despise any form of ḥalāl employment even though it may be a humble one.

~

1 Jawāhir Pāre, vol 1, p 90

Appreciating the countless blessings of Allāh ﷻ produces contentment of heart. Complaining makes life dull and unpleasant for oneself and others.

بسم الله الرحمن الرحيم

Hope in Allāh's ﷻ Mercy

A king was afflicted with a severe life-threatening ailment. The physicians who were attending to him, all concurred that no medicine could cure him. His only hope of survival was to transplant the organs of a young boy into his body. The king agreed and made an announcement that such a young boy be found. After much searching, they found a young boy who matched the description provided by the physicians. The parents were bribed with a colossal sum of money and agreed to hand over their son. The corrupt judge of the time passed his verdict of acceptability. He reasoned that the life of a young boy could be taken to save the life of the king.

As the executioner was about to proceed, the young boy raised his gaze to the heavens and smiled.

The king was surprised and asked, "How can you smile when your life is about to be taken?"

The boy replied, "Young boys place their hopes upon their parents. Disputes are resolved by judges. Justice is dispensed by kings. In my case, my parents have sold my life for a pittance, the judge has passed his verdict of death and the king sees his pleasure in my suffering. In such a condition, I see no hope, but in that Being who is Pure and Elevated."

The king was overcome by the golden words of the young boy, and with tears is his eyes, he declared, "My death is better than taking the life of this innocent boy." He then embraced the boy, kissed his forehead and set him free with a handsome reward. Within a week, the king also recovered fully from his illness.[1]

A person whose focus is upon the mercy of Allāh سبحانه وتعالى finds pleasure and success in situations which others regard as hopeless.

~

An oppressor always fails because Allāh's سبحانه وتعالى pleasure and mercy accompanies the oppressed.

بسم الله الرحمن الرحيم

Trustworthiness of the Highest Order

Moulānā Muḥammad Munīr رحمة الله عليه was one of those fortunate souls who participated in the wars waged against the British while fighting for Indian independence. He also served as the fourth principal of Dārul ʿUlūm Deoband. His sense of honesty and trustworthiness was absolutely outstanding. On one occasion Moulānā travelled to Delhi in order to print the annual Madrasah review. Unfortunately, the money which he had brought with him on behalf of the Madrasah was stolen from him. Moulānā did not inform anybody of the theft. He quietly returned home and sold one of his private properties. He then took the equivalent amount that was stolen from him and returned to Delhi to complete the printing. A few days later, the news somehow leaked out within the Madrasah. A number of the senior teachers decided to inform Moulānā Rashīd Aḥmad Gangohī رحمة الله عليه of the matter and requested his verdict. Moulānā Gangohī رحمة الله عليه explained that the money was a trust in the hands of Moulānā Muḥammad Munīr رحمة الله عليه. As he had not displayed any negligence in the loss thereof, he could not be held accountable. The staff approached

1 Jawāhir Pāre, vol 1, p 261; Gulistān

Moulānā Muḥammad Munīr and showed him the verdict of Moulānā Gangohī. They requested him to take back the money he had given from his side.

Moulānā Muḥammad Munīr read it and remarked, "Has Moulānā Rashīd Aḥmad Gangohi studied fiqh and issued this verdict for my sake? Moulānā Gangohī should place his hand upon his heart and ask whether he would have taken back the money if he had been in a similar situation. I do not accept the verdict and I will never take back the money that I have given."[1][2]

Our pious predecessors set an outstanding example of diligence and trustworthiness in dealing with public funds.

بسم الله الرحمن الرحيم

Blinded by Wealth

One day, Shaikh Abul ʿAbbās Al-Mursī set out from Madīnah Munawwarah to visit the grave of Hamzah. A stranger noticed the Shaikh and decided to follow him. As they approached the grave, a door leading to the enclosure miraculously opened without a key. As the Shaikh entered, he noticed some people whom he had never seen before. He realised that these were men from the unseen and seized the opportunity to make duʿā' to Allāh. He asked Allāh for forgiveness, ease and contentment in this world and the Hereafter.

The Shaikh continues, "Out of compassion I requested my companion to also ask from Allāh what his heart desired, as we had found the hour of acceptance. The man made duʿā' to Allāh to grant him a dinār. As we

1 Jawāhir Pāre, vol 1, p241

2 In terms of the Shariah, the verdict was correct and it was permissible for Moulānā to take back the money. However, due to his high level of sincerity he refused to accept it.

returned to Madīnah, a man approached us and handed my companion a dinār. I then proceeded to meet my spiritual mentor, Sayyid Abul Ḥasan Ash-Shādhilī. Before I could explain what had transpired he said to my companion, "You were fortunate to have found the hour of acceptance of duʿās, but all you requested was a dinār! Why did you not request for forgiveness and contentment like Abul ʿAbbās?"[1]

Prayers and words are an expression of the heart. One whose heart is inclined towards Allāh ﷻ, always remembers the Hereafter, while one who is attached to the world seeks only its riches.

One Last Business Trip

Shaikh Saʿdī رحمة الله عليه narrates: I once met a businessman who owned a hundred and fifty camels and employed forty servants and slaves. One night, he led me into his small private chamber. He did not sleep the entire night, nor did he allow me to do so. His discussion revolved around futile talk concerning his business life, "Such and such of my goods are in Turkey and part of my wealth is in India. This is the deed of sale for such and such property of mine. So and so has so much of my wealth in trust," he explained.

He then continued with his confused hopes and aspirations, "I want to travel to Alexandria. The climate is perfect there. But, the only problem is that the ocean on the Western coast causes floods."

He continued, "Listen Saʿdī, I also intend embarking on a serious business trip. If this trip proves a success I will retire and settle down for the rest of my life."

1 Jawāhir Pāre, vol 1, p207; Mirqāt

I asked, "What business trip is that?"

He continued, "I hope to travel to Iran and purchase sulphur which I hope to export to China. I have heard that sulphur will bring me a fortune in China. From China, I will purchase dinner sets, which I hope to export to Rome. From Rome, I will export silk to India. From India I will export iron to Aleppo. From Aleppo, I will export mirrors to Yemen. From Yemen I will export shawls to Paris. Thereafter, I will quit travelling and settle down into a shop."

The businessman continued with his perplexing hopes and ideas at such length that I did not have the opportunity to utter a single word. After much frivolous talk, he looked up at me and asked, "Saʿdī, why don't you relate some of your experiences to me?"

I answered, "Did you hear about the wealthy man who fell from his horse last year? His dying words were, 'Only contentment or the sand of the grave can fill the eyes of a person who is infatuated with the riches of the world.' "[1]

A man who is overcome with greed for worldly riches is neither happy nor content. His dreams of growing his empire will terminate when he is put to rest in his grave. Then only will the reality of his folly dawn upon him.

Mutual Respect

A woman from Delhi had the habit of frequenting the home of her parents. Her husband, who was not in favour of her leaving his home on a regular

1 Jawāhir Pāre, vol 2, p206; Gulistān

basis, finally issued her a warning, "In future, if you go to your father's home, you are divorced from me."

Soon thereafter, her father passed away and they were left in a precarious situation. She could neither proceed to the funeral home for fear of being divorced from her husband, nor could she absent herself from her father's funeral.

Her husband presented his case before a leading scholar of the time, Shāh ʿAbdul ʿAzīz رحمة الله عليه. He explained, "If your wife proceeds to her father's home, she will certainly be divorced from you." Upon hearing the answer, the husband felt totally despondent and began to weep.

Incidentally, Qādhī Thanā'ullāh Pānipatī رحمة الله عليه, a student of Shāh ʿAbdul ʿAzīz رحمة الله عليه, was present and listened to the discussion intently. After hearing his teacher's explanation he respectfully said, "Most honourable teacher, I think that the divorce will not take place, since the passing away of her father has caused the ownership of the house to be transferred to his children. Since he no longer owns the house, she will not be divorced by entering it."

Shāh ʿAbdul ʿAzīz رحمة الله عليه was amazed with the variant opinion of his student and accepted it with a smile on his face.[1]

Couples need to be cautious with regard to their choice of words. A few moments of uncontrolled anger can easily result in a lifetime of regret.

~

Differences amongst intellectuals are natural. When such differences are based on authentic knowledge, sincere intentions and respectful presentation they are a source of strength and goodness. However, when such differences are based on paltry knowledge, insincerity or presented in an impolite manner, they fuel the fires of enmity and conflict.

1 Jawāhir Pāre, vol 1, p 223

Marital Harmony

A scholar who was once delivering a sermon mentioned: "When a person intends giving Ṣadaqah, seventy Shayāṭīn[1] prevent him from doing so by clamping down on his hands, feet and heart."

A devotee from amongst the gathering heard these words and proclaimed, "Today, I will fight and overpower these seventy Shayāṭīn." With determination and resolve, he left the Masjid and returned home, where he began to fill a bag with wheat. As he was about to leave to distribute it as Ṣadaqah, his wife realised his intention and caught hold of him. She began to convince him to abandon the idea, but he refused. A quarrel ensued between them and she eventually succeeded in snatching the bag from his hands. The man returned to the Masjid, dejected and defeated.

As he entered the scholar asked, "What happened?"

He replied, "I defeated the seventy Shayāṭīn quite easily, but their mother arrived on the scene and defeated me!"[2]

While the concluding statement of the husband should not be taken too seriously, the incident is typical of many a home where conflict is the order of the day. To be successful in any good venture, both the husband and wife are required to strive in unity and harmony. When either of them is overpowered by false intentions they become a stumbling block to progress.

1 Plural of Shaiṭān.

2 Tafsīr Ar-Rāzī, Vol 1, p 101; Jawāhir Pāre, vol 1, p 142

A Blessed Death

Shāh ʿAbdul ʿAzīz Muḥaddith Dehlawī رحمة الله عليه narrates: “When I resided in Delhi, I came to know about a female servant who was quite elderly. She was uneducated with regard to even the basics of Islām, and was irregular with her Ṣalāh due to her old age and weak physical condition. She, however, commanded the respect of her offspring and her family members, who saw to her needs with great care and dedication.

When she was on her deathbed, she began muttering some words in her Eastern Urdu accent, but nobody could understand what she was trying to convey. A number of the learned and righteous men in the neighbourhood were called, but none could make any sense of her utterances. Finally, they called Shāh Ahlullāh رحمة الله عليه, my uncle. After listening to her, he deciphered the words,

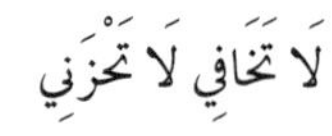

“Do not fear, nor be sad.”

Shāh Ahlullāh رحمة الله عليه requested her caretakers, “Enquire why she is uttering these words.”

After a great deal of effort, she explained that a group of angels had arrived and were reciting these words, which were now upon her tongue as well. Shāh Ahlullāh رحمة الله عليه then asked whether she understood the meaning of these words.

She replied, “Not really, but I can sense that these are angels that have come to console me.”

Shāh Ahlullāh رحمة الله عليه requested, “Enquire from her regarding the action she had performed on account of which she is being consoled at this time.”

After some time, she replied, “These men gathered around me are saying that I do not have any real good deeds to my credit. However, one day I went to the market to purchase some melted butter. When I returned home I boiled it, and to my surprise, found a rupee in the pot. My initial reaction was to keep it, as nobody knew about it, but I realised that Allāh was watching me. I returned the rupee to the owner of the shop. These men are now saying that my action of returning the rupee was so beloved to Allāh that they were sent to me at this critical time of my demise to give me glad tidings."[1]

No good deed should be considered insignificant. Allāh ﷻ often showers His choicest blessings due to actions which common men regard as trivial.

~

The realisation that Allāh ﷻ is All-Knowing is sufficient as a motivation towards doing good and abstaining from evil.

بسم الله الرحمن الرحيم

The Blessing of an Educated Wife

Muftī ʿAbdul Qayyūm رحمة الله عليه was the Muftī of his time when he resided in Bhopāl, India. When dealing with social issues, he was often called upon to deliver a verdict. At times, he could not arrive at a clear answer based on the teachings of Islām. Without any hesitation or fear of being labelled, he would casually say to the disputing parties, "Please bear with me a minute." Sometimes, he would openly proclaim, "Wait a moment, while I seek the opinion of my wife."

He would then walk into his home and discuss the matter with his wife, who was the daughter of Shāh Isḥāq رحمة الله عليه, a scholar of high repute. He would ask her whether she had heard any Ḥadīth from her father

1 Jawāhir Pāre, vol 1, p 156

regarding the matter and what her opinion was. He would then return and deliver his verdict.[1]

Fortunate are those couples who are blessed with the opportunity of jointly serving humanity, due to the knowledge which Allāh ﷻ has blessed them with.

~

Wise parents invest in the religious and spiritual nurturing of their offspring.

~

One of the greatest bounties that a man can have is a righteous wife.

بسم الله الرحمن الرحيم

Abstention from Interest

Yazīd ibn Hārūn رحمه الله was once asked, "When will a Muslim scholar reach the rank of being able to deliver fatāwā (Islāmic verdicts)?"

He replied, "When a scholar reaches the rank of Imām Abū Ḥanīfah."

The questioner was amazed at the answer and asked, "What are you saying?"

Yazīd ibn Hārūn رحمه الله replied, "I am prepared to take it a step further and say that Imām Anu Ḥanīfah رحمه الله is the greatest and most righteous Muslim jurist that I have ever seen. One day, I noticed the Imām sitting outside the door of a person in the full heat of the sun. I suggested that sitting in the shade of the wall of the house would be more comforting for him. He replied, "The owner of this house owes me some money and I, therefore, regard it as improper to benefit from him in any way.""

1 Jawāhir Pāre, vol 1, p 177

In another narration of this incident, Imām Abū Ḥanīfah رحمة الله عليه further explained, "As the owner is indebted to me, I regard my benefiting from the shade of his house as makrūh (reprehensible). I would not like to derive any benefit from my creditor."

Imām Abū Ḥanīfah رحمة الله عليه probably had the following Ḥadīth of Nabī ﷺ in mind:

كل قرض جر منفعة فهو وجه من وجوه الربا

"Any such loan which derives some benefit for the lender, is a form of ribā (interest)." (Sunan Al-Bayhaqī).

~

Righteous men of the past detested ribā (interest) to the extent that they would abstain from dealings which had even the slightest possibility of doubt. A stark contrast indeed to today's greedy society where interest transactions are regarded as the norm!

بسم الله الرحمن الرحيم

Winning Hearts

During the Khilāfah of 'Umar رضي الله عنه, a man from Syria, who was strong and firm in stature, used to visit Madīnah regularly. After some time, he stopped and 'Umar رضي الله عنه noticed his absence. Upon enquiry, 'Umar رضي الله عنه was informed that his condition had taken a bad turn as he had become an alcoholic. 'Umar رضي الله عنه summoned his scribe and dictated the following letter:

من عمر بن الخطاب إلى فلان ابن فلان، سلام عليك، فإني أحمد إليك الله الذي لا إله إلا هو غَافِرِ الذَّنْبِ وَقَابِلِ التَّوْبِ شَدِيدِ الْعِقَابِ ذِي الطَّوْلِ لَا إِلَهَ إِلَّا هُوَ إِلَيْهِ الْمَصِيرِ

"From ʿUmar ibn Khaṭṭāb to so-and-so person. May peace be upon you. For your benefit, I praise that Allāh, Who is the one and only deity worthy of worship. He forgives sins, He accepts repentance, He is severe in punishment and He is All-Powerful. There is no deity worthy of worship besides Him and to Him is the return."

ʿUmar ﷺ then gathered his companions and requested them, "Make duʿā' for so-and-so person that Allāh opens his heart to accept the truth and that Allāh forgives him."

When the letter reached him, he read it repeatedly, pondering over its message. He was eventually reduced to tears and committed himself to abandoning his drinking. Allāh ﷻ granted him the ability to give up the evil habit for good.

When ʿUmar ﷺ heard the news, he wisely advised his companions, "This is how you should handle cases of this nature. If you notice a Muslim brother involved in sin, then rectify and encourage him. Make duʿā' to Allāh to forgive him. Do not approach him in a manner whereby you become an accomplice of Shaiṭān."[1]

A golden piece of advice for those involved in propagation and counselling. The core of a well-balanced invitation to the truth should consist of encouragement, motivation and genuine concern for the well-being of people.

1 Tafsīr Ibn Kathīr, vol 12, p 168; Jawāhir Pāre, vol 2, p129;

Conquering Hearts with Good Character

A fire-worshipper owed a sum of money to Imām Abū Ḥanīfah رحمه الله. One day, Imām Abū Ḥanīfah رحمه الله decided to request for payment, and set out to meet him at his home. As he approached the door, he unknowingly stepped upon some impurity, which stuck to his shoe. In his attempt to shake it off, a portion of it landed up on the wall of the fire-worshipper's home. The Imām now found himself in a dilemma.

"If I leave it on the wall, it will result in an unpleasant stain," he thought, "and if I scrape it off, the sand will be removed. In either case, the wall will be damaged."

Still pondering over his predicament, he knocked on the door and a servant opened. The Imām advised her to inform her master that he was waiting at the door. The fire-worshipper arrived and, thinking that the Imām had come to claim his dues, began to make excuses.

Imām Abū Ḥanīfah رحمه الله immediately stopped him and said, "Never mind the debt, a matter of greater importance has developed." He then explained what had occurred with the wall and asked, "How do we clean it without damaging it further?"

The fire-worshipper was amazed at the Imām's concern for his well-being and replied, "Before purifying the wall, I prefer to purify my soul." With these words he accepted Islām.[1]

Seeing to the well-being of others often touches the cords of the heart and leads to the triumph of truth and goodness. On the other hand, being oppressive, hurtful or inconsiderate draws the wrath of Allāh ﷻ and the enmity of man.

1 Tafsīr Al-Rāzī, vol 1, p 241; Jawāhir Pāre, vol 2, p 232

بسم الله الرحمن الرحيم

Reformation of a Murderer

The sage, Khwājah Muʿīnuddīn Chishtī رحمة الله عليه was a paradigm of forbearance and compassion. One day, an evil-minded person arrived at the home of the sage with the intention of killing him. The sage received the news of the man's intention, and decided to welcome him with a great deal of respect and kindness. As the man drew closer the sage received him warmly and requested him to be seated.

He then calmly said to him, "I know why you have come. You may proceed with your objective." When the man heard this, he was totally overawed and began to shake.

When he had regained his composure he timidly explained, "I was sent to kill you and have been promised a great reward in this regard." He then produced a dagger which he threw down in front of the sage, and began to weep.

"Take your revenge!" he exclaimed, throwing himself at the feet of the sage.

Khwājah Muʿīnuddīn Chishtī رحمة الله عليه explained, "It is a principle of the sages that we counter evil with good. When a person harms us, we display kindness to him. Until now, you have not harmed me in anyway." The sage then lifted his hands in duʿā' for the man, who, by this time, was completely won over. He remained in the service of the sage for a lengthy period of time. On one of his many Ḥaj trips he passed away and lies buried in the blessed lands.[1]

Compassion and good character transforms enemies into friends, whereas harshness and vulgarity transforms friends into enemies.

1 Jawāhir Pāre, vol 2, p 212

Escapism as a form of Deception

Yazīd ibn Abī Ḥabīb ﷫ was a Tābiʿī and one of the three Muftis who were appointed in Egypt by ʿUmar ibn ʿAbdul ʿAzīz ﷫. On one occasion, he was ill and the governor of Egypt arrived to pay him a visit. In the course of their discussions, the governor asked a question, "Is the Ṣalāh of such a person valid, whose clothing is stained by the blood of a mosquito?"

The pious man heard the question and turned his face away in displeasure. He remained silent for the remainder of the visit. Finally, as the governor rose to leave, Yazīd ibn Abī Ḥabīb ﷫ remarked, "You are responsible for shedding the blood of so many of your subjects almost on a daily basis, yet you have the audacity to ask regarding the blood of a mosquito!"[1]

A common disease of the soul is to escape from the reality of one's wrongs by means of disguise or evasion. A true seeker of truth should be brave enough to acknowledge his weaknesses and rectify them. A coward often clouds the horizon with superfluous issues. Such a person only deceives himself by attempting to fool others. No matter how hard he tries, he can never escape from Allāh ﷻ, the All-Knowing.

An Amazing Answer

A person once took an oath to perform such an *ʿibādah* (form of worship) which no other person in the entire world could perform at the same

1 Jawāhir Pāre, vol 2, p 301; Tadhkiratul Ḥuffāẓ, vol 1, p 130

time as himself. If he did not succeed in performing such an *ʿibādah*, his wife would be irrevocably divorced from him. The ʿUlamāʾ of the time were presented with the case and requested to provide a solution to his dilemma. They were all astounded and could not think of any such act of worship.

When Shaikh ʿAbdul Qādir Jīlānī رحمة الله عليه, the sage of the age, was approached he immediately explained, "The Maṭāf around the Kaʿbah should be vacated and he should be allowed to perform seven Ṭawāfs individually."

The ʿUlamāʾ were astonished with the answer and agreed that Ṭawāf was the only *ʿibādah* through which his oath could be fulfilled, since it may only be performed at one location on earth."[1]

May Allāh ﷻ reward the learned scholars of Islām for their dedication, sincerity and tremendous service to the Muslim Ummah by providing amazing and practical solutions to complex issues.

~

A husband should be cautious of the words that he utters. Words take a few seconds to utter, but often have far-reaching implications.

بسم الله الرحمن الرحيم

Thought-provoking Words on a Tombstone

Dāwūd عليه السلام used to spend a considerable amount of his time in the mountains where he would make dhikrullāh[2] in abundance. One day, while walking, he found himself at the mouth of a cave. To his amazement, he saw an enormous corpse spread out on the floor. Close to the head of

1 Jawāhir Pāre, vol 3, p 280; Tārīkh Daʿwato ʿAzīmat

2 The remembrance of Allāh ﷻ.

the corpse, there was a tombstone with the words: "My name is King Waisam. I ruled for one thousand years, during which period I conquered one thousand cities. I defeated one thousand armies and married one thousand princesses. Despite all my accomplishments, my end result is before you. Sand is my covering and a stone is my pillow. Now that you have seen my condition, ensure that the life of this world does not deceive you."[1]

The intelligent ones do not squander their time and efforts in the quest of power, riches and worldly pleasures.

بسم الله الرحمن الرحيم

The Eid of 'Umar ibn 'Abdul 'Azīz رحمة الله عليه

Ramadhān was almost over and the streets of Damascus were buzzing with a sense of happiness in preparation for the day of Eid, which was only a few days away. The days were hot, but the bazārs were crammed with delicacies and people. Men, women and children, mostly from the wealthier families, filled the market place anxiously searching for the best deals on offer. A few streets away, the son of 'Umar ibn 'Abdul 'Azīz رحمة الله عليه, the Khalīf of the time, ran into his home crying. The boy's mother instinctively picked him up in her arms and wiped away his tears.

"Why are you crying my dear? Did anybody say something to hurt you?" she asked. But the boy's sobbing only increased.

Again she tried, "I told you not to fast because of the heat. Many boys who are older than you are not fasting. Why do you try to fast when you are so young? I am sure that the heat has drained you, and you are crying out of thirst?"

1 Jawāhir Pāre, vol 3, p 114; Al-Kanzul Madfūn

Between his sobs, the boy explained, "Mother, I promise you in Allāh's name that I am not thirsty, nor has the fast weakened me."

"Then why are you crying?" she asked and continued, "Eid is only a few days away. You should be looking forward to attending the Eidgāh with your father. You know that Eid is a day of joy."

"But," the boy explained, "this is the reason why I am crying. I know about Eid. All my friends, whose father's are courtiers and ministers of my father, will be present at the Eidgāh, dressed in new clothing."

His mother replied, "You do not need to worry, as I will wash your old clothing with my own hands."

The boy continued, "But, mother, all my friends have bought fine new clothes and I am feeling shy about my old clothes. I do not want to go to the Eidgāh." With these words the boy again burst into tears. His mother understood her son's request and felt sorry for him. "I will try my best, my dear. Why don't you sleep for a while," she consoled him.

Shortly thereafter, ʿUmar ibn ʿAbdul ʿAzīz رحمة الله عليه, returned home having completed his administrative duties of the Khilāfah. As he was about to lie down for a nap, his wife approached him, "Amīrul Mu'minīn, may my life be sacrificed for you. Eid is approaching and our son is anxious to have a new set of clothing. He arrived home crying about it, and I advised him to sleep for a while."

The Khalīf lowered his head and said, "You are well aware that I only receive a monthly salary of a hundred dirhams. With this we purchase our food and pay for the services of a servant. We barely succeed in coming out every month. Rarely do we consider purchasing clothing because the salary is just sufficient for our basic expenses. As far as the public treasury is concerned, the money rightfully belongs to the poor, destitute, orphans and widows. I am only a custodian who has been entrusted to distribute it to the deserving ones. To even think of utilising this wealth is a sin."

"I agree fully, my beloved husband, but the boy does not understand why he has to dress in old clothing while his friends have the best. He has been so deeply saddened by this that you can still notice the stains of tears on his cheeks."

The husband advised, "Fāṭimah, if you have any personal goods of value, perhaps you should sell them and please him by using the proceeds to purchase a new set of clothing for him."

She answered, "Amīrul Mu'minīn, you have already placed all my jewellery in the public treasury. You even placed the valuable necklace given to me by my father in the public treasury. Besides the love and obedience I have in my heart for you, I have nothing left."

'Umar ibn 'Abdul 'Azīz رحمه الله again lowered his head and began to ponder deeply. He began to reflect about his past, his childhood, his youth and the luxuries he enjoyed while growing up. He recalled those days when he would not wear an outfit more than once. He recounted the times when the streets where he walked would be perfumed for hours with the scent he wore. He possessed numerous sets of clothing which would lay untouched in his closet. The memories brought tears to his eyes. His wife was saddened at his condition and began to apologise, but he said to her, "Don't worry, Fāṭimah, I was just recalling the days of my youth."

He then wrote a letter and handed it over to his servant, saying, "Take this to the officer in charge of the public treasury. Take extreme care of whatever he gives you and bring it to me." In the letter he requested that he be given a month's salary in advance. The servant left, but returned a few moments later empty-handed. The servant handed a letter from the treasurer to the Khalīf. It read: "O Khalīf of the Muslims, I can fulfil your request with ease, but are you certain that you will live for a month? If not, then why are you taking the rights of the poor, the orphans and the widows onto your shoulders?"

The Khalīf read the letter and with tears in his eyes, remarked, "My honourable treasurer, you have surely saved me from a calamity."

The day of Eid arrived and the streets and homes of Damascus were buzzing with joy. People proceeded to the Eidgah dressed in their newly purchased outfits. 'Umar ibn 'Abdul 'Azīz رحمه الله also set out holding the hand of his son. Each of them wore an old set of clothing which had been carefully washed. The young boy's face shone brightly, as he walked alongside his father, convinced that the eternal pleasures and comforts of Jannah are far superior to the temporary beauty and adornment of this world.[1]

Our righteous and pious predecessors chose the path of simplicity for themselves and their families, despite the many painful sacrifices they had to endure.

بسم الله الرحمن الرحيم

Defending a Woman's Honour

ʿUmūriyyah was the most fortified city of the Roman Empire and the powers of the day were unsuccessful in conquering it. The Muslim Khalīf, Muʿtaṣim Billāh, was one day sitting amongst his courtiers and ministers discussing various issues, when a man briskly walked into the assembly. He explained that he had just returned from Rome, and the Khalīf questioned him about prevailing conditions over there.

He explained, "I cannot report anything out of the ordinary, except one nasty scene which I witnessed one particular day. I was walking through the bazārs of ʿUmūriyyah when I noticed an Arab female purchasing an item from a local trader. Unfortunately, the deal turned sour and they began arguing. Finally, the trader slapped the woman forcefully, breaking a number of her teeth. Instinctively the woman cried out,

وا معتصماه

"O Muʿtaṣim! Help me!"

The man mockingly remarked, "Do you ever think that your Khalīf can assist you here?"

1 Jawāhir Pāre, vol 3, p 147

This was the only unfortunate incident I witnessed during my stay in the Roman lands."

After hearing the incident, Muʿtaṣim was overcome with rage. His eyes reddened, as he stood up and proclaimed,

لبيك ايتها المراة المسلمة

"O Muslim woman, I will come to your aid."

Without any further delay, he set out with his army. Upon reaching ʿUmūriyyah, he launched an attack on the city and conquered it. He then had the guilty person arrested and the Muslim woman was afforded the opportunity to regain her honour."[1]

Muslim leaders of the past would prepare armies to defend the honour of a single woman. Nowadays, many Muslim leaders have been blinded by superficial power and wealth and choose to ignore the cries of countless oppressed Muslim women and children.

بسم الله الرحمن الرحيم

Generosity of the Highest Order

Imām Ḥasan, Imām Ḥusain and ʿAbdullāh ibn Jaʿfar ﷺ were proceeding for Ḥaj when the camel on which their provisions were loaded suddenly ran off. They continued walking in a state of hunger and weakness. Fortunately, they stumbled upon a tent, occupied by an old woman. They enquired whether she could oblige with some drinking water or milk, to which she replied in the affirmative.

1 Jawāhir Pāre, vol 3, p 152

After they had dismounted from their camels, she pointed to a lean goat, saying, "You may milk the goat and drink therefrom." After doing so, they asked if she had any food from which they could partake.

She replied, "Yes, this very goat. One of you may slaughter it and I will cook it for you." They complied with her offer and ate the meal she laid out before them.

As evening drew closer, they addressed her again, "We are from the family of Hāshim and we are proceeding for Ḥaj. If Allāh returns us safely to our homes in Madīnah after Ḥaj, we invite you to pay us a visit. We would like to recompense you for your generosity and kindness upon us." With these words they proceeded on their way.

That night, the old woman's husband returned home and she explained her encounter with the three men.

But, her husband reprimanded her angrily, "How could you sacrifice our goat for a group of strangers? You have no idea who they really were."

She explained that they were from the noble Arab family of Hāshim. The husband was not satisfied with her answer, but did not pursue the matter further.

As the days passed, their condition deteriorated and the couple was compelled to come to Madīnah, where they could seek employment. During the day, the woman would walk the streets to gather camel droppings and later sell them as fertilizer. One day, as she was doing her rounds, she passed by the home of Ḥasan ﵁ who immediately recognised her. He quickly called his servant and instructed him to call her.

When she arrived, Ḥasan ﵁ asked, "O servant of Allāh, do you recognise me?"

She replied, "No."

He continued, "I was one of those guests to whom you had shown kindness by serving milk and cooking the meat of a goat."

The old woman could not believe this and asked, "Are you really the same person?"

He replied, "Yes, I am." He then instructed his servants to purchase a thousand goats and handed them over to her. He then gave her an additional thousand dinārs in cash. He also instructed his servant to direct her to the home of his younger brother, Ḥusain ؓ.

When she arrived there, Ḥusain ؓ asked her how his brother, Ḥasan ؓ, had compensated her.

She replied, "A thousand goats and a thousand dinārs in cash."

Ḥusain ؓ similarly compensated her with a thousand goats and a thousand dinārs and directed her to the home of ʿAbdullāh ibn Jaʿfar ؓ. He also asked her how the two brothers had compensated her, and then gave her two thousand goats and two thousand dinārs. He explained further, "Had you come to me first, I would have given you even more."

She returned to her husband with her four thousand goats and four thousand dinārs and remarked, "This is the compensation I have received for our lean goat."[1]

The intelligent are extremely generous in repaying a kind gesture.

بسم الله الرحمن الرحيم

A Fortunate Mother

Lubābah رضي الله عنها gave birth to six sons while married to ʿAbbās ؓ. Their names were Faḍl, ʿAbdullāh, ʿUbaidullāh, Quthm, ʿAbdur Raḥmān and Maʿbad ؓ. In addition to the fact that they were all Ṣaḥābah, they all passed away in remote lands. Faḍl passed away in the lands of Shām. The narrations vary regarding his exact cause of death. Some say that he was martyred during battle, while others opine that he was caught in a plague. ʿAbdullāh passed away in Ṭā'if around the year 70 Hijrī. ʿUbaidullāh, according to

1 Jawāhir Pāre; vol 3, p 189; Iḥyā ʿUlūmuddīn

the majority of historians, passed away in Madīnah during the Khilāfah of Yazīd. Quthm passed away in Samarqand, during the Khilāfah of Muʿāwiyah ﷺ while travelling with Saʿīd ibn ʿUthmān ﷺ. His grave in current day Uzbekistān is known as Shāhe Zindā. ʿAbdur Raḥmān and Maʿbad were martyred during the Khilāfah of ʿUthmān ﷺ while in Africa. They were in the army of ʿAbdullāh ibn Saʿd ibn Abī Sarḥ and were buried in Tunis in the year 26 Hijrī.[1]

A mother who is focussed on earning the pleasure of Allāh ﷻ, raises her sons to serve the religion of Islām.

بسم الله الرحمن الرحيم

Ṣadaqah Eradicates Disease

A water-well

A person once approached the distinguished scholar of Ḥadīth, ʿAbdullāh ibn Mubārak رحمة الله عليه and said, "I have a boil on my knee for the last seven years. I tried numerous medications and consulted several doctors, but have had no success."

ʿAbdullāh ibn Mubārak رحمة الله عليه advised, "Search for a community wherein the inhabitants are in need of water and have a water-well dug there. I have faith that, as the water begins to gush forth from that land, your wound will heal." The man did as he had been advised, and was cured through the grace of Allāh ﷻ.

1 Jawāhir Pāre, vol 2, p 256

A pond

Imām Baiḥaqī رحمة الله عليه narrates that his teacher, Imām Abū ʿAbdullāh Ḥākim رحمة الله عليه, was once afflicted with a severe rash of pimples on his face. He tried various forms of treatment, but none brought any relief.

After a year had elapsed, he requested Imām Abū ʿUthmān Aṣ-Ṣābūnī رحمة الله عليه, "Please make duʿā' for my cure during your Friday teaching session." The request was fulfilled and that Friday the Imām, together with his students, sincerely focussed their attention towards Allāh سبحانه وتعالى and beseeched Him to cure the Imām.

The next Friday, an elderly woman approached the gathering of Imām Abū ʿUthmān رحمة الله عليه and handed him a letter which read, "Last Friday, I heard the duʿā' you had made for Imām Abū ʿAbdullāh Ḥākim. When I returned home, I too begged Allāh to cure him. That night, I saw Nabī ﷺ in a dream, saying to me, "Advise Abū ʿAbdullāh to provide water for the benefit of the Muslims."

The Imām took the letter and presented it to Abū ʿAbdullāh. Upon reading through it, he immediately instructed that a pond be constructed in front of his home. This was done, and ice was placed in the water to cool it. People then began to drink therefrom.

Imām Baihaqī رحمة الله عليه continues, "Within a week, the signs of acceptance were already visible on his face. The pimples soon vanished and he was completely cured."

Ṣadaqah eradicates illnesses and calamities.

In a Ḥadīth, Nabī ﷺ also advised, "Protect your wealth with Zakāt, cure your sick with Ṣadaqah and avert calamities with duʿā'."[1]

1 Majmaʿuz Zawā'id, Jawāhir Pāre, vol 2, pg 28; At-Targhīb Wat-Tarhīb

بِسْمِ اللهِ الرَّحْمٰنِ الرَّحِيْمِ

A Khaṭīb[1] Admonishes a Khalīf

The Khalīf of Andalus, An-Nāṣir, was extremely fond of fine buildings and architecture. In this regard, he would spend much time in acquiring the latest knowledge and skills from other areas. He would spare no effort in seeking the means to immortalise his kingdom and prestige. His preoccupation with this led him to build the famous Madīnatuz Zahrā'. His strength and energy were totally exhausted in its decoration and perfection. He became so engrossed, that he failed to attend three successive Jumuʿah (Friday) prayers at the Jāmiʿ Masjid. Qādhī Mundhir ibn Saʿīd رحمة الله عليه, the *khaṭīb*, decided to admonish him so that he would repent from his ways. He began his sermon by quoting a verse from the Qur'ān,

أَتَبْنُوْنَ بِكُلِّ رِيعٍ آيَةً تَعْبَثُوْنَ وَتَتَّخِذُوْنَ مَصَانِعَ لَعَلَّكُمْ تَخْلُدُوْنَ وَإِذَا بَطَشْتُمْ بَطَشْتُمْ
جَبَّارِيْنَ فَاتَّقُوْا اللهَ وَأَطِيْعُوْنِ وَاتَّقُوْا الَّذِيْ أَمَدَّكُمْ بِمَا تَعْلَمُوْنَ أَمَدَّكُمْ بِأَنْعَامٍ وَبَنِيْنَ
وَجَنَّاتٍ وَعُيُوْنٍ إِنِّيْ أَخَافُ عَلَيْكُمْ عَذَابَ يَوْمٍ عَظِيْمٍ قَالُوْا سَوَاءٌ عَلَيْنَا أَوَعَظْتَ
أَمْ لَمْ تَكُنْ مِنَ الْوَاعِظِيْنَ

"Do you build high palaces in vanity. And do you acquire for yourselves fine buildings in the hope of living therein forever? And if you seize by force, do you seize as tyrants? So fear Allāh, and obey me. And fear Him Who has aided you with all that you know. He has aided you with cattle, sons, gardens and springs. Verily, I fear for you the punishment of a Great Day. They said: 'It is the same to us whether you preach or not.'" (*Sūrah Ash-Shuaʿrā', verse 128-136*)

He then recited another verse of the Qur'ān,

1 A person who delivers the Jumuaʿh sermon.

قُلْ مَتَاعُ الدُّنْيَا قَلِيْلٌ وَالْآخِرَةُ خَيْرٌ لِمَنِ اتَّقٰى

"Say: The enjoyment of the world is little. The Hereafter is better for one who fears Allāh." (Sūrah An-Nisā', verse 77)

He then continued to explain that the life of the Hereafter was one of permanence and genuine rewards. Eloquently, but frankly, he rebuked those who focussed all their attention on the construction of elaborate buildings. He cautioned against becoming engrossed in decorating them and squandering vast sums of money on them. He continued in this vein and substantiated his advices with verses from the Qur'ān,

أَفَمَنْ أَسَّسَ بُنْيَانَهُ عَلَى تَقْوٰى مِنَ اللهِ وَرِضْوَانٍ خَيْرٌ أَمْ مَنْ أَسَّسَ بُنْيَانَهُ عَلٰى شَفَا جُرُفٍ هَارٍ فَانْهَارَ بِهِ فِي نَارِ جَهَنَّمَ وَاللهُ لَا يَهْدِي الْقَوْمَ الظَّالِمِيْنَ

"Is he who has laid the foundation of his building upon piety to Allāh and His pleasure better, or he who has laid the foundation of his building on the brink of a precipice ready to crumble, so that it crumbled with him into the Fire of Hell! And Allāh does not guide those who do wrong." (Sūrah At-Tawbah, verse 109)

The Qāḍhī warned about the suddenness of death and invited his audience towards abstinence from this fleeting world. He encouraged them to curtail and limit their attachment to the world and avoid fulfilling their lusts and desires. With each of these thoughts, he recited the appropriate verse from the Qur'ān and mentioned a Ḥadīth of Nabī ﷺ. His words had a tremendous impact upon the audience. Many acknowledged their wrongs, shed tears, prayed, submitted and repented to Allāh ﷻ. The Khalīf was most affected. He realised that the words of the sermon were directed at him. He cried out of remorse for his past deficiencies and sought Allāh's ﷻ protection from His wrath. This was despite his dislike for Mundhir's direct approach.

After Mundhir رحمة الله عليه had departed, he complained to his son, Al-Ḥakam, "Mundhir directed his sermon to me specifically. He exceeded the bounds in his criticism of me. In advising me, he did not choose his words wisely. He violently shook my heart and it was as if he was prepared to strike me with his staff." Burning with rage, he promised that in future, he would perform Ṣalāh behind Aḥmad ibn Muṭarraf in Qurṭuba instead of Mundhir.

Al-Ḥakam asked, "If you dislike him, why do you not replace him with another Imām to lead the Ṣalāh?"

Upon this, An-Nāṣir rebuked and reprimanded Al-Ḥakam, saying, "Can any person equal Mundhir ibn Saʿīd in piety and knowledge? Should he be removed for the pleasure of one who is diverted from the truth? This should never happen. I would be ashamed to face Allāh ﷻ and have a person besides the righteous and truthful Mundhir as a mediator between me and Him in Jumuʿah Ṣalāh. However, he has put me through difficulty and I have unfortunately taken an oath. I wish I had the ability to atone for my oath. We can never replace him and he will continue leading the Ṣalāh, if Allāh ﷻ wills."

Al-Ḥakam later apologised for his statement against Mundhir, saying, "O Amīrul-Mu'minīn, he is a righteous man. He desired only good through his sermon."[1]

Foolish are those who focus all their efforts on constructing mansions and palaces in this temporary life. Wise are those who focus their attention towards the eternal life of the Hereafter.

~

Muslim scholars and Imāms are fully entitled to speak out against the evils of their rulers and should do so fearlessly when the need arises.

1 Nafḥuṭ Ṭīb Min Ghuṣnil Andalus Ar-Raṭīb, p 570

A Strange Thief

Ibn Mājishūn رحمة الله عليه was a distinguished scholar of the Mālikī school of thought. One day, a friend of his came to visit and explained, "Today I had a unique encounter. I was walking towards my orchard when a stranger suddenly confronted me, demanding, "Remove your clothing!"

I enquired, "Why?"

He replied, "Because I am your brother and do not have any clothing."

I asked in astonishment, "What type of a brother makes a demand of this nature?"

He replied, "You wore these clothes for a predestined period of time. Now it is my turn to wear them."

I then asked, "Do you want me to remove these clothes and become naked?"

He replied, "I have heard a Ḥadīth narrated by Imām Mālik رحمة الله عليه that performing ghusl (regulatory bath) whilst in the nude is permissible, and you are proceeding to perform ghusl."

I asked, "But are you also requesting me to be naked in public?"

He replied, "This is a secluded place. Had I known that people would be passing by, I would not have made such a request."

I requested, "At least allow me to reach my orchard. From there I will send these clothes to you after removing them."

He replied, "Never! Once you reach your orchard, I suspect that you will send your servants to capture me."

I assured him, "No, I promise that I will not do so."

He continued, "I know that a promise made to a thief is null and void."

I pleaded, "I take an oath that I will send them to you willingly."

He waited a while and then answered, "I reflected upon the lives of all the thieves since the era of Nabī ﷺ, but I could not recall any of them dealing with their victims on credit. I, therefore, do not desire to introduce such a bidʿah (innovation)."

His explanation left me speechless. I removed my clothing and handed it over to him."[1]

When a man is blinded by sin, he will resort to the most ridiculous explanations and proofs to justify his wrongs.

~

Incorrect or partial understanding of Islāmic teachings is harmful.

بسم الله الرحمن الرحيم

From a Criminal to a Saint

Baghdād was the capital of the world in terms of knowledge and civilization around the fourth century after Hijrah. However, as history has repeatedly illustrated, uncontrolled progress in the material world often brings along with it a host of social and moral problems. Luxuries and wealth attracted the criminal element and resulted in an increase in theft, looting and highway robberies. Just as Baghdād was famously associated with saints like Junaid Baghdādī رحمة الله عليه, it also produced the likes of notorious criminals like Ibn Sabāt. Ibn Sabāt was known as the kingpin of crime in Baghdād and feared by many.

Little is known about his youth. He was initially arrested for theft at the age of fifteen for stealing from a bakery. Investigations revealed that he was not from Baghdād. He was born in a city called Das. While on a journey to Baghdād, both his parents passed away. He was brought to Baghdād by a caravan and unfortunately, got caught up with the wrong crowd. For his first offence, he was given a moderate punishment and

1 Kitābo Ki Darasgāh Me, p 79

released. Unfortunately, he returned to a life of crime and, with time, he became bolder and more ferocious in his attacks.

Soon the magnitude and brutality of his crimes worsened and he turned towards larger businesses, wealthier households, gold and jewellery. He became a leader of a criminal syndicate which began to attack and rob at will. Highway robberies, house and farm burglaries and even attacks upon state institutions were carried out with meticulous detail and precision. The inhabitants were completely stunned with his ingenuity.

But, Ibn Sabāt was fortunately apprehended. One day, he was the last of the group to escape. The police arrived in time to arrest him. He was caught in the act and was handed the death sentence. But, his horrid occupation had robbed him of all honesty and shame. When he realised that his end was close, he resorted to a deceptive scheme. He suggested to the state that if they spared his life, he would lead the police to all the criminals he knew and have them arrested. They agreed. He was saved, but over a hundred from his own syndicate were arrested and killed. Curses could be heard emanating from the lips of each of his accomplices as they were killed. Now, he had proved that he was a violent criminal who was even prepared to betray his very own. He completed a jail sentence of ten years and was released.

Baghdād was silent one dark night as the inhabitants were all asleep. Suddenly, out of the darkness, there was a movement. A man began to walk from one gully to the next. He finally stood before a house and looked up into the night sky. A significant part of the night had already passed, and he wondered how long he would still have to search. This was the same Ibn Sabāt, who resumed his criminal activities on the first night after his release. Carefully, he surveyed the situation. He noticed a large wall with a gate.

"This house is probably inhabited by a wealthy person," he thought to himself and stepped forward. He tried the handle of the gate and amazingly found that it was open. In a second he opened it and stepped in. As he approached the porch, he noticed an open space in the middle with small rooms all around. One room appeared larger than the rest, and he walked towards it. Amazingly, this door was also left unlocked, almost as if a visitor was being anticipated. He opened it and stepped in. Here he found himself in a fairly large hall. His eyes did a quick visual inspection of the room to determine if there were any contents of value. He noticed a mat made of date palm leaves at one end and a pillow made of leather lying at the other. In a corner, a number of shawls made of coarse clothing lay scattered. Close by, lay a few topis (hats) made of wool.

He thought to himself, "This is my first night out, and I have come to a place where there is nothing of real value. How foolish is the inhabitant and trader that resides in this house! Does he not know how to conduct a business? He has such a mansion, but has nothing of real value therein!" He began to curse and abuse the owner in his mind, realising that the only items he could take were the shawls, even though they were of little value. In addition, they were heavy and he had only one hand to gather and carry them. He picked up one of the shawls and deliberated over its weight and the effort required in carrying it. "These shawls should rightfully be carried upon the backs of mules," he thought.

But, the night was almost over and he could not consider the idea of breaking into another home. He had no time to waste and decided to take whatever he could. He laid out one of the shawls and placed therein as many as he could carry. Now, he ran into another problem. The material was coarse and thick and he found it difficult to tie it up into a bundle with his single hand. He tried using his foot and then his teeth, but his efforts were in vain. The darkness of the room added to his problems. Soon he was exhausted and frustrated by his inability and misfortune.

All of sudden, he heard the noise of a person walking softly. For a while, it was quiet, and then he became conscious of a person standing at the door of the room. Ibn Sabāt quickly sat up. Almost in an instant, the door opened and a man stood before him. In his hand he held a lantern which illuminated every corner of the room. The man was dressed in a long robe which was tied around his waist with a cloth. On his head he wore a long black hat. He was very lean and thin and appeared slightly hunched, as he stood. Despite his stature, Ibn Sabāt noticed that his face showed no sign of suffering. Instead, it displayed clear signs of serenity, perseverance and a beauty which he could not explain. The man gazed at Ibn Sabāt for a few moments, and then stepped forward with a slight smile on his face, almost as if he had understood the situation.

After a few more moments, he quietly said, "My friend, what you are attempting to do cannot be done easily without any light. I am here to help and we can gather these items easily together." As he was about to bend he suddenly stopped and said, "I notice that you are tired. Your forehead is dripping with perspiration. The room is hot and dark. How difficult it must be for you to earn your sustenance in this manner. Here, I am laying down this mat and the pillow against the wall. Relax a bit, while I complete your work." With these words, he gently placed his hand on the shoulder of Ibn Sabāt and motioned him to sit down. He untied a handkerchief from his waist, and wiped away the perspiration from the brow of Ibn Sabāt, who noticed his eyes shining with fatherly love.

The events had unfolded so rapidly that Ibn Sabāt did not have the chance to reflect on what was transpiring. He sat down on the mat, totally surprised and confused. He began to observe the old man as he opened the loosely-tied bundle. He spread out two of the shawls on the ground and began placing the others onto them. He then closed them up and tied each one in the form of a bag. All of this was done with total serenity and ease. For a while, the man stood still as if he had remembered something. He stood up, removed his own shawl and placed it with the others in the bundle. He then approached Ibn Sabāt and said, "My friend, I notice from your face that you are not only tired but also hungry. If you can wait a few moments before leaving, I will bring you some milk to drink." His smile was powerful enough to melt the hardest of hearts and before Ibn Sabāt could reply, the man left the room.

Ibn Sabāt found himself alone, but could not gather the strength to rise to his feet. The conduct of the strange man had not frightened him, but he was surprised. His presence and awe had filled the space and time leaving Ibn Sabāt without a moment to reflect. Now that he was alone, the reality of the situation slowly began to dawn upon him. Never before had he experienced such uncertainty. Questions began to enter his mind: "What is going on here? Who is this man? Surely he could not be the owner of the house as thieves are not accustomed to receiving such a warm reception from owners. But who was he, then?"

Suddenly, a new thought dawned upon him. "How foolish I have been! The matter is as clear as daylight," he thought. "This is another thief. Perchance we both chose the same location. He is probably from the area and knows that the house was going to be empty for the night. He, therefore, arrived with a lantern and is going about his work completely relaxed. He will in all probability divide the loot between us."

The opening of the door brought his thoughts to a halt. Again, the man appeared, holding a large wooden cup in his hands. "I have brought you some milk. Drink it! It will be beneficial for your hunger and thirst." He placed the cup in the hand of Ibn Sabāt, who drank it in a single gulp.

Now, Ibn Sabāt spoke up firmly, "Look! I was here before you and according to our principles, I deserve to take all of this. However, I am prepared to share it with you, but remember that your share will be less than mine."

The stranger did not reply. He only smiled. Thinking that he was unhappy with the suggestion, Ibn Sabāt stood up angrily and screamed, "You fool! Why don't you answer me? Do you think that you can fool me with a glass of milk and a few kind words? Do you know who I am? You can never fool me! I have fooled the entire world. Speak! Are you happy with my suggestion or not? If not, then..."

The stranger's lips began to move, but the smile was still on his face, "My dear friend! There is no need to get upset? Let us complete the job before us. You carry the smaller bundle as you have only one hand. I will take the larger one. Regarding the matter which has upset you, I do not want to discuss it now. As you have indicated that you wish to work with me, I too would like to work with you."

"Fine, if you agree with me then we can proceed. At this moment, you do not know who I am, but remember that you will not find a better supervisor than myself," Ibn Sabāt exclaimed, and assisted the stranger to place the heavy bundle on his back.

Despite Ibn Sabāt's displeasure at the stranger's boldness, he could not hold back his amazement, "You appear to be quite lean, but you display amazing strength in carrying a load!"

But within, he thought, "His physical strength does not match his intelligence. How foolish of him to carry my share which is the heavier of the two. If I did not run into a fool like this, I would have had to suffice on only two shawls for the night."

Ibn Sabāt picked up his small bundle and they left the house. The stranger's back was now totally bent due to the weight of the load. Ibn Sabāt was in a hurry and insisted that they quicken the pace. The man tried his best to follow the order, but the weight subdued him. The shawls were just too heavy. More than once, did the stranger stumble and almost fall over, but he continued walking without a word.

But, Ibn Sabāt was not contented. As his command to increase the pace bore no fruit, he resorted to verbal abuse. They arrived at a bridge which began with an incline. The stranger could not handle the slope and fell to the ground. As he tried to stand up, Ibn Sabāt rushed to his side and kicked him violently, screaming, "You dog! If you cannot carry the load, why did you bring it?"

The stranger stood up gasping for breath. Instead of anger or displeasure, his face displayed signs of embarrassment. He quickly picked up the bundle and began walking. Now, they had reached the outskirts of the city, which were largely deserted. They arrived at a dilapidated house and Ibn Sabāt instructed, "Leave the bundle here!" He jumped through an opening and ordered the stranger to throw in the two bundles. The stranger then entered. They proceeded into an underground room which Ibn Sabāt had settled into since his release from prison. They were silent for a while and then Ibn Sabāt took a step towards the stranger. The night had almost passed and the first of the morning light began to penetrate into the enclosure. Now Ibn Sabāt could see the stranger properly. He had a broad smile on his face. He had not spoken for two hours and now explained, "I have completed my services and would like to return. I am sincerely embarrassed about my incompetence and the inconvenience that I have caused you. I apologise for this and hope that you will forgive me. In this world, forgiveness of each other's shortcomings for the sake of Allāh should take priority over other matters. Before I leave you, I need to tell you one thing. I am not whom you suspect I am. I am the owner of the house where we had met and you chose my company. Every night I spend some time in that particular room where I found you. You were an honoured guest in my home and I am sorry that I could not serve you better. You know where I reside and you should feel free to come to me if you require any further assistance. May the peace of Allāh be upon you and may you be showered with His blessings!" With these words, he shook Ibn Sabāt's hand and left.

Ibn Sabāt was now in a world of his own - a world of total amazement and confusion. As he looked at the stranger walking away, he did not know how to react. Meanwhile, the streets of Baghdād were filled with people, proceeding for Fajr. Soon thereafter, the day's activities commenced with labourers and businessmen proceeding to work. But Ibn Sabāt remained seated where he was. His gaze was fixed on the two bundles before him, as if he was searching for his strange companion within them.

Hours passed by, but Ibn Sabāt remained motionless, deep in thought. He did not realise his hunger. His fear of daylight left him. All he could think of, was the strange man whom he had met the previous night. His life had only been one of evil, lies, murder, theft and deception. This was the first time he had ever experienced love, mercy, kindness and sacrifice. His life had been one of worldly attachment, but now he realised that there was another realm in which this world faded into oblivion. Now, the veils were removed and his eyes were opened to the reality of life. He could not fathom how a man could assist others in such a kind manner, without expecting a reward for his efforts.

He repeatedly thought to himself: "This was not a thief like me. He was the owner of the house! Rather than arrest me and have me punished, how did he deal with me?" He went through the incident in his mind over and over, pondering over the strange man's manner and words. As he recalled them each time, they pierced his heart and soul.

"I went as a thief to steal his wealth. I considered him to be a thief. I swore at him. I forced him to the ground and hurt him. But how did he respond to me?"

The sun was now setting and the sound of the Maghrib Adhān could be heard from the Masājid minārets of Baghdād. Ibn Sabāt rose, wore his shawl and walked out into the street. The fear that had previously filled his heart, had now given way for another emotion. He walked towards the house where he had been the previous night. It did not take him very long to find it. Close by, he noticed a small house which belonged to a woodcutter. He approached the man and asked, "Which trader resides in this house opposite the road?"

The woodcutter asked in surprise, "Trader? I can see that you are not from the area. This is not a trader's dwelling. Shaikh Junaid Baghdādī resides here."

Ibn Sabāt had heard the name, but was not well-acquainted with the personality. He walked to the door, which was open like before. As he peeped in, he noticed the straw mat, the pillow and thirty to forty people sitting around a man. This was Shaikh Junaid Baghdādī! At that moment, the Adhān for 'Īshā' went off and the people rose to prepare for Ṣalāh. The Shaikh rose, and as he reached the door, Ibn Sabāt fell to his feet in humility and repentance. The Shaikh raised him to his feet and looked at him. Ibn Sabāt's eyes flowed with tears but his lips were motionless. There was no need for speech now. When the eyes of the heart are opened then the tongue does not need to speak.

Soon Aḥmad ibn Sabāt joined the company and lessons of Shaikh Junaid Baghdādī رحمة الله عليه and was transformed into a saint of Allāh سبحانه وتعالى.[1]

A few moments of love and kindness can convert a hardened criminal into a saint.

بسم الله الرحمن الرحيم

A Deceitful Thief Meets His Match

Abū Ja'far Muḥammad ibn al-Faḍl as-Samīrī narrates: "A pious old woman used to live in our village. She would fast excessively and perform Nafl

1 Kitābo Ki Darasgāh Me, p198

Ṣalāh in abundance. Unfortunately, she had a son who earned a living by dealing in interest and was heavily involved in gambling and consuming liquor. By day, he would attend to his business and around evening time, he would return home and hand over the money he had earned, to his mother for safekeeping. His nights were spent in sin and vain pleasures.

One day, a thief decided to steal his money. He quietly followed him home and entered the house without difficulty. He then concealed himself and waited. The young man handed the bag of money to his mother and left the house. She placed it in a particular room, wherein all their other valuables were also kept. The room was reinforced with solid timber walls and the door was made of iron. She then sat down in the same room and partook of her meal after the day's fast. The thief thought to himself that she would soon lock up the room and retire for the night and he could then emerge from his hiding place, open the door and take the bag. To his dismay, she remained where she was and began to perform Ṣalāh. She prolonged the Ṣalāh to such an extent that half the night passed. The thief was agitated and soon began fearing that she would continue her worship till daybreak. He quietly began searching the house and soon laid his hands upon a cloth and a string. He tied the cloth around his waist and lowered himself down a stepladder. From there, he called out in a loud tone in order to frighten the old woman. But, she was wise and immediately realised he was a thief.

Giving the impression that she was afraid she asked in a nervous voice, "Who are you?"

The thief answered, "I am Jibra'īl. I have been sent by the Lord of the worlds to guide your son. I have been instructed to advise him so that he abandons his sinful ways."

In an uneasy tone the old woman requested, "Jibra'īl, I beg you to be kind to him as he is my only son."

The thief replied, "I have not been sent to take his life."

"But why have you been sent then?" she asked.

"I have been instructed to take away his bag of money so that he is grieved by the loss. He will then repent and I will then return his money."

The old woman continued, "Fine, you may proceed with your order."

He then requested, "Please step aside from that door." She complied.

He then entered the room and began gathering all the valuables. The old woman quietly shut the door, and tied the lock, trapping him in the room. The thief realised that he was now in a predicament and desperately began searching for an opening to exit from the room, but there was none.

Frantically, he cried out, "You may now open the door as your son has accepted my advice."

The old woman replied, "Jibra'īl, I am afraid that your celestial beauty will blind my eyesight."

"I will extinguish my celestial beauty so that it does not harm you," he tried to reassure her.

But she persisted, "Jibra'īl, what prevents you from exiting through the roof or flying over the walls with the aid of your wings? In this way, my eyesight will not be threatened."

Now, the thief realised that he was dealing with a wise old woman. He endeavoured to soften her by apologising and repenting, but she ignored him.

"You will have to remain in the room until morning," she exclaimed and resumed her Ṣalāh. He continued pleading until sunrise when her son returned. She related to him what had happened. He summoned the police who promptly arrived and arrested him.[1]

Those who are gullible often fall prey to fraudsters, but not those who are equipped with knowledge and wisdom.

1 Latā'ife 'Ilmiyyah, p306

Appreciating Good Character

Al-Ḥasan ibn Ismāʿīl was once seated with his companions, discussing the qualities and noble character of Imām Aḥmad ibn Ḥanbal رحمة الله عليه. He explained, "I heard my father saying that over five thousand people would frequent the discourses of the Imām. From them, only about five hundred would come to record the Aḥādīth he narrated. The remainder would come to learn his excellent conduct and noble character."

Abū Bakr ibn al-Muttawwiʿī also corroborated this by stating, "I attended the gatherings of Imām Aḥmad ibn Ḥanbal رحمة الله عليه for twelve years, while he taught the Musnad to his offspring. I did not write a single Ḥadīth. I would only watch his conduct, character and demeanour."[1]

A true scholar teaches by his conduct and actions, not only his words.

بسم الله الرحمن الرحيم

Suspicion

Ḥasan Baṣrī رحمة الله عليه once noticed a slave with a woman near the banks of the River Tigris. In his hand, the slave held a bottle from which he was drinking. The saint thought to himself, "I regard myself as a sinner, but I am superior to this slave."

As he looked on, a boat with seven men on board began to sink in the river. The slave instantly jumped into the water and saved six of them. He then turned to the saint and remarked, "I have saved six of the seven.

1 100 Qissah wa Qissah Min Ḥayāt al-Imām Aḥmad ibn Ḥanbal, p 17

Since you regard yourself as superior to me, I request that you save the remaining person on the boat."

He then explained, "I was trying to test you to see if you were blind or observant. This woman by my side is my mother and the bottle in my hand contains nothing but water."

Ḥasan Baṣrī ﵀ realised his error and immediately begged the man for forgiveness. He also requested, "Just as you saved six men from drowning, save me from drowning in the sea of blindness." From then onwards, Ḥasan Baṣrī ﵀ never regarded anybody with contempt.[1]

One should strive to develop the quality of humility.

بسم الله الرحمن الرحيم

A Disciplined Disciple

Bāyazīd Busṭāmī ﵀ remained in the company of Imām Jaʿfar Aṣ-Ṣādiq ﵀ for his spiritual nurturing. One day, while sitting, the Imām requested, "Bāyazīd, please stand up and hand me that particular book from the shelf."

Bāyazīd Busṭāmī ﵀ asked in astonishment, "What shelf?"

The Imām exclaimed, "You have stayed with me for such a long time, yet you do not know of a bookshelf in my home."

Bāyazīd Busṭāmī ﵀ explained, "Since I have been in your company, I have not had the courage to raise my gaze, hence I do not know of the bookshelf. I did not come here to waste my time."

The Imām was impressed with his disciple and instructed, "Return to Busṭām. You have completed your training in my company."[2]

---

1 Tadhkiratul Awliyā, p 30

2 Tadhkiratul Awliyā, p95

One who seeks to refine his character should develop humility and respect.

بِسۡمِ اللّٰهِ الرَّحۡمٰنِ الرَّحِيۡمِ

Knowledge Draws Honour

Hashīm ibn Bashīr was born in Bukhārā, but relocated to Baghdād. His father earned his living as a chef. Hashīm loved knowledge from a very tender age and had no inclination towards cooking. His family, on the other hand, disliked his quest for knowledge. Despite their objections, he continued studying. He began attending the Ḥadīth lessons of Qādhī Abū Shaibah رحمة الله عليه, a renowned muḥaddith of Baghdād. Naturally, his enthusiasm and regular attendance caught the eye of his teacher. One day Hashīm fell ill and could not attend the lesson. The muḥaddith enquired about his whereabouts and was informed accordingly.

"In that case, let us visit and console him," he said to his students, and they all set out for the humble home of Bashīr, the chef.

They sat for a while and then departed. Bashīr then turned to his son and remarked, "Son, I used to prevent you from acquiring the knowledge of Ḥadīth, but I will refrain from doing so in future. The barakah of knowledge was the only reason for bringing the Qādhī to my door. I would have never dreamt of such an honour had this not been the case."[1]

Knowledge acquired for the pleasure of Allāh ﷻ attracts numerous blessings and benefits, one of which is to spend time in the company of the pious.

1 Kitābo Ki Darashgāh Me, p185

بسم الله الرحمن الرحيم

The Fruits of Determination

Ustādh Yūsuf Dehlawī was a renowned calligrapher, who was incredibly gifted in the art of calligraphy. It is reported that there was once a handwriting contest close to the banks of the Jumna River. Many calligraphers arrived at the sandy banks of the river, including Ustādh Yūsuf. He began writing with a large bamboo stick and when he had completed writing from alīf[1] to shīn[2] of the alphabet, he had already covered a distance of one furlong (about 200 meters). People then requested him to stop.

He then addressed his audience, "Colour in the letters and then take a photograph of it from an aeroplane. I am quite certain that the image will be identical to the original I have drawn here." Nobody gathered the courage to challenge his work further on that day.

Once a person asked Ustādh Yūsuf from whom he had learnt the art of calligraphy. He replied, "I had no teacher. My father was a renowned calligrapher, but I did not learn the art from him."

Upon further enquiry he explained, "I learnt the art from the Lāl Kila (Red Fort), where I noticed the calligraphic works that dated back to the Mughal Empire. They were engraved with the best and finest calligraphy of the time."

Ustādh Yūsuf would go to the Lāl Kila everyday and memorise the design of a couplet. He would then return home and continue drawing what he had memorised, until he was pleased with his work. The next day, he would take his paper drawings and return to the Lāl Kila where he would compare them with the original and correct any mistakes. He continued with this practice for a period of ten years. His enthusiasm and ardent desire for perfection made him an outstanding calligrapher of his time.[3]

---

1 & 3 Letters of the Arabic alphabet.

3 Kitābo Ki Darasgāh Me, p170

A person who has a firm desire to achieve something in life will pursue his goal with zeal and determination.

~

Practice makes perfect.

Abstaining From Incomprehensible Issues

Imām Muzani رحمه الله narrates: "Whenever I was in doubt regarding any matter, I would request an explanation from Imām Shāfiʿī رحمه الله. Once, a question regarding tawḥīd (Oneness of Allāh) arose in my mind. I approached Imām Shāfiʿī رحمه الله while he was seated in a Masjid in Egypt, and said, "A question regarding tawḥīd has been troubling me and I know that nobody, except you, will be able to answer it."

Imām Shāfiʿī رحمه الله replied in a somewhat troubled tone, "Do you realise where you are seated?"

"Yes," I replied.

Imām Shāfiʿī رحمه الله continued, "You are in the land where Allāh ﷻ drowned Firaʿwn. Have you ever come across any Ḥadīth in which Nabī ﷺ posed such a question?"

"No," I answered.

Imām Shāfiʿī رحمه الله then asked, "Did any of the Ṣaḥābah pose such a question?"

"No," I answered.

Imām Shāfiʿī رحمه الله asked, "Do you know how many stars there are in the sky?"

"No," I answered.

Imām Shāfiʿī رحمه الله asked, "Do you know how many planets there are? Do you know the various types of planets, the rising and setting of each and what they are composed of?"

"No," I answered.

Imām Shāfiʿī رحمه الله continued, "When you do not even have adequate knowledge about those things which are visible to you, why do you want to enter into a discussion regarding their Creator?"

He then asked me a question regarding wudhū. I answered it incorrectly. He then continued to pose four related questions. I could not answer any of them correctly.

He then explained, "You are required to fulfil this obligation five times a day and you have not acquired sufficient knowledge regarding it. You have rather chosen to dwell into the subject of the Being of Allāh! In future, if such a question arises in your mind then hand the matter over to Allāh and focus upon the following verse:

> *And your God is one God; there is no God but He, Most Gracious Most Merciful. Verily, in the creation of the heavens and the earth, and in the alternation of night and day, and the ships which sail upon the sea with that which is of use to mankind, and the rain which Allāh sends down from the sky and thereby bringing to life an earth that was dead, and the creatures of all kinds that He has scattered therein, and in the changing of winds and clouds which are held between the sky and the earth, are indeed signs for people of understanding. (Sūrah Baqarah, verses 163-164)*

In this way, use the creation to reach the Creator and do not pursue such issues which are beyond your intelligence. From then onwards, I made taubah and refrained from engaging in such matters."[1]

A sign of maturity and wisdom is to master the basics. Strange is the thinking of those who ponder over matters which are difficult to

1 A'immah Arbaʿah Ke Dilchasp Wāqiʿāt, p230

comprehend, while remaining oblivious of those issues for which they are accountable.

بسم الله الرحمن الرحيم

A Mother's Golden Advice

When Imām Mālik ibn Anas رحمة الله عليه was still a young boy, he said to his righteous mother, "I desire to go out and acquire knowledge."

His mother dressed him as a student of knowledge, placed a turban upon his head and gave him some advice before he left, "Now go to Rabī'ah, but learn his good character and conduct before you begin to learn the knowledge he dispenses."[1]

A person who acquires book knowledge, but does not refine his character can never attain the status of the true scholars.

بسم الله الرحمن الرحيم

Wisdom of Allāh's سبحانه وتعالى System

Masrūq رحمة الله عليه narrates: "A bedouin owned a dog, a donkey and a rooster. The rooster used to wake up the household for Ṣalāh. The donkey was used to transport their water and tents, while the dog would guard them. One day, a fox devoured the rooster. The family was saddened at the loss, but the man who was endowed with piety, remarked, "There is goodness in this."

1 Tartībul Madārik vol 1, p 130; 100 Qissah Wa Qissah Min Ḥayāt al-Imām Mālik, p 5

After some time a wolf attacked the donkey and killed it. Again the family was saddened but the pious man remarked, "There is goodness in this."

Thereafter, the dog was killed. Again the pious man remarked, "There is goodness in this."

Some time later, a robbery took place in their neighbourhood. All their neighbour's homes were burgled, but the home of the bedouin was spared.

They then realised the goodness that Allāh ﷻ had planned in the deaths of their animals. The thieves had stolen from the other homes because they had heard animal noises emanating from them and thought that they were wealthy households. The bedouin's home had no animals, hence it did not attract the attention of the thieves who thought that their home had nothing of value.[1]

Man often fails to grasp the wisdom of the divine, but needs to develop a firm conviction that everything happens by the command of Allāh ﷻ and has inherent goodness therein. Acceptance of this divine system produces contentment of heart.

Scholar Teaches a Lesson in Humility

Eid had arrived and the takbīr and taḥlīl echoed through the streets of Madīnah. The Amīr of Madīnah, ʿAbdul Malik ibn Ṣāliḥ, emerged boastfully clad in armour and surrounded by guards and flags.

When Imām Mālik رحمة الله عليه noticed this, he displayed his displeasure and remarked,

1 Anīsul Mu'minīn, p88

إِنَّا لِلّٰهِ وَإِنَّـا إِلَيْهِ رَاجِعونَ

To Allāh do we belong and to Him is our return.

Nabī ﷺ and the righteous khulafā' did not behave like this."

His statement reached the ears of the Amīr, who approached the Imām at the Eidgah and asked, "What do you dislike regarding us?"

Imām Mālik رحمة الله عليه replied, "I find this conduct of yours reprehensible. People should attend Ṣalāh in humility and desirous of attaining the forgiveness of Allāh. Yaḥyā ibn Sa'īd narrated to me that Nabī ﷺ entered Makkah during the conquest at the head of ten or twelve thousand men, but his head was lowered. Upon his lips were the words, "

الْمُلْكُ لِلّٰهِ الْوَاحِدِ الْقَهَّارِ

The kingdom belongs to Allāh, the One, the Irresistable.

Nabī ﷺ would proceed to the Eidgāh and the Ṣalāh of Istisqā leaning on a staff or spear, while his head was lowered in humility."

'Abdul Malik ibn Ṣāliḥ was embarrassed when he heard the golden words of advice from the scholar.[1]

Pomp and power do not blind the righteous from expressing the truth.

بِسْمِ اللهِ الرَّحْمٰنِ الرَّحِيمِ

Allāh's سبحانه وتعالى Planning is Absolute

Dhunnūn Miṣrī رحمة الله عليه narrates: "I was once on a journey and the earth was white with snow. I noticed a fire-worshipper, who had covered his head, sprinkling some bird-seeds on the ground."

1 Tartībul Madārik vol 2, p104; 100 Qissah Wa Qissah Min Ḥayāt al-Imām Mālik, p 70

In surprise, I asked, “What are you doing?”

He replied, “The snow has covered the land entirely and the birds would find it extremely difficult to find food. I am, therefore, sprinkling some seeds for them to eat so that mercy may descend upon me.”

I remarked, “Seeds from strangers are not acceptable in the divine court!”

He explained, “Even if this is not accepted, I would be content if my action is being watched.” I was amazed at his courage.

Some time later, I proceeded for Ḥaj and noticed the fire-worshipper enthusiastically performing Ṭawāf of the Ka‘bah. When he saw me, he remarked, “Allāh ﷻ noticed my action and accepted it. In return, He has granted me His recognition and has drawn me close to Him. He has also invited me to His House. I am exceptionally pleased at this point.”

He then turned his attention towards prayer and supplicated, “O Allāh, in return for a handful of bird-seeds You invited a fire-worshipper to Your House. You are most generous.”

Immediately, we heard a voice from the unseen, saying, “Allāh ﷻ does not require a reason to invite or prevent anybody from visiting His House. Remain content as you are. Allāh does as He pleases. His planning is beyond your intelligence.”[1]

Allāh’s ﷻ planning is beyond human control and comprehension.

بسم الله الرحمن الرحيم

Honour and Disgrace

One day, the Khalīf Mahdī’s wife, Khaizarān, was seated in the palace together with a number of other females when one of her servants arrived

1 Tadhkiratul Awliyā’, p88

with the message that a woman from a noble family was at the door. She was extremely poorly dressed and was requesting permission to enter. She did not state her name or provide the reason for her visit. Khaizarān instructed the servant to allow her to enter. Despite her tattered clothing, the signs of nobility were visible from her features.

Khaizarān asked, "Sister, who are you?"

She replied, "I am Muznah, the wife of Marwān ibn Muḥammad (the last of the Ummayad Khulafā'). I have been reduced to this pitiable condition you see me in presently, due to the passage of time. Even the clothing I am wearing was acquired by begging. Despite my desperate condition, my noble family lineage does not permit me to interact with the common people. I have come to your door so that my condition may not be exposed to all."

Khaizarān heard the words and her eyes filled with tears. But Zainab, who was quite close to Khaizarān and was known to talk a lot, spoke out, "Muznah! Have you forgotten that day when we came to you in Harrān and requested that you hand over the body of Imām Ibrāhīm to us? You reprimanded us and chased us away, saying that women have nothing to do with men's matters. Instead, your husband, Marwān, gave us a better hearing when we approached him. He took a false oath that he had not killed Imām Ibrāhīm, and handed the body over to us. He even offered to assist us financially, but we refused the offer."

Muznah replied, "By Allāh, this pitiable condition of mine is the result of our actions at that time. You are encouraging Khaizarān to follow the incorrect path which we followed then. You should rather be encouraging her towards good and not towards revenge. In this way, the bounties that you enjoy will remain with you and Islām will remain strong. Sister Zainab, you have noticed how Allāh has already punished us in this world for our evil dealings, yet you do not have compassion for us." With these words, she began to cry uncontrollably. Khaizarān was deeply affected by her words, but did not want to oppose Zainab, and hence kept her emotions concealed. Discreetly, she indicated to a servant to lead Muznah into one of the royal chambers and have her cleaned up and dressed suitably.

When the Khalīf Mahdī arrived, Zainab had already left. He spent some time with his wife, as was his daily habit, and she recounted the day's proceedings to him. Khalīf Mahdī immediately summoned the servant and asked what Muznah had said when she was led to the chamber. She replied, "With tears streaming down her cheeks she recited these verses:

وَضَرَبَ اللَّهُ مَثَلًا قَرْيَةً كَانَتْ آمِنَةً مُّطْمَئِنَّةً يَأْتِيهَا رِزْقُهَا رَغَدًا مِّن كُلِّ مَكَانٍ فَكَفَرَتْ
بِأَنْعُمِ اللَّهِ فَأَذَاقَهَا اللَّهُ لِبَاسَ الْجُوعِ وَالْخَوْفِ بِمَا كَانُوا يَصْنَعُونَ

And Allāh presents the parable of a city which was secure and content, its provision coming to it in abundance from every place, but it ungratefully denied the favours of Allāh. So Allāh made it taste the extremes of hunger and fear because of that (evil) which they (its people) used to do. (Sūrah Naḥl, verse 112)

When the Khalīf heard this, he burst into tears and turned to Allāh in du'ā':

"O Allāh, I seek Your protection from the removal of bounties."

He then turned to Khaizarān and exclaimed, "If you do not deal kindly with Muznah then you should never speak to me again. Had Zainab not been one of our elderly females, I would have taken an oath to sever all communication with her. He then summoned a female servant and sent his greetings to Muznah with the following message: "Beloved cousin, at present all your sisters in faith are with me. I would have come to you in person if it would not have been difficult for you."

Muznah understood the message and immediately came to the Khalīf, who welcomed her. He asked her to be seated and consoled her regarding the desperate condition her family had been reduced to.

He explained, "Had I been comfortable marrying in your family, I would have married you. As this is not possible, I would advise you to maintain your ḥijāb in my presence and remain with your sisters in the palace. You will be treated with dignity just like them." He then instructed that she be treated with kindness and equity.

Muznah remained in the palace in happiness and ease for the remainder of her life. She passed away during the Khilāfah of Hārūn Ar-Rashīd.[1]

Allāh ﷻ raises and relegates the status of people according to their actions.

بِسْمِ اللّٰهِ الرَّحْمٰنِ الرَّحِيْمِ

Fighting Dogs

Aḥmad ibn Ammār narrates: "A group of students set out together with their teacher to attend a janāzah. As they proceeded, they noticed a pack of dogs playing happily together. The teacher turned to his students and remarked, "Notice how happily these dogs are playing together."

After returning from the janāzah, they again passed by the dogs. This time, however, they were standing around a carcass and barking at each other. They then began to bite and snatch morsels of meat from the carcass. Within a short time they were growling and fighting with each other over the meat.

The teacher turned around to his students and warned, "My students, you have seen these animals. Remember that you too will remain the best of friends as long as worldly riches do not come between you. When the world comes between you, you too will argue and fight like dogs over a carcass."[2]

1 Jawāhir Pāre, p 64; Murūjudh Dhahab

2 Tārīkh Dimishq Vol 5, p 85; 170 Qissah Wa Qissah Lil Ḥāfiz Ibn ʿAsākir p103

Short-sighted men whose gaze is upon the material world are often driven by greed to quarrel, fight and even kill.

Prioritise

ʿAbdullāh ibn Qāsim, who was the scribe of ʿAbbās ibn Aḥmad ibn Tūlūn, narrates: "Aḥmad ibn Tūlūn called for me at around midnight. I responded, uncertain and fearful regarding the summons at such a late hour. The messenger led me to a dark room which I entered.

I greeted Ibn Tūlūn and he returned my greeting. "What is the purpose of this room?" he asked still sitting in the darkness of the room.

I replied, "To ponder and think."

"Why?" he asked.

I replied, "There is nothing of value herein to divert one's attention."

"Well done! Now proceed to my son, ʿAbbās, and instruct him to come to me in the morning. Ensure that he does not consume anything until he comes to me. I would like him to have meals with me."

I replied, "To hear is to obey," and left.

The next morning I came to ʿAbbās and did as Ibn Tūlūn had ordered. ʿAbbās would become very impatient while hungry and he insisted on eating something before we left to see his father, but I objected and prevented him from doing so. We arrived and were seated. Ibn Tūlūn delayed in presenting the meal, until he was convinced that his son's hunger was intense. Eventually, when the food was brought, there was nothing but cold cooked vegetables. ʿAbbās immediately began to devour them and ate to his fill. His father watched him intently and did not touch the food. He then ordered that the remainder be removed. In a few minutes, other dishes were laid out. These consisted of a variety of chicken, mutton and lamb. Ibn Tūlūn began to eat. He invited his son to join him, but he could not eat even a morsel as he was satiated.

Ibn Tūlūn then advised his son, “I put you through this trial to teach you a lesson. Do not indulge yourself or utilise your energy in minor matters as these will distract you from the major issues. Issues of minor importance will drain your resources, preventing you from utilising them in issues of greater importance.”[1]

Those who are not focussed upon the bigger picture often get lost in trivial and irrelevant matters.

Justice towards a Christian Woman

During the Khilāfah of ʿUmar ibn Khaṭṭāb ﷻ, a Christian woman from Egypt complained to him that her house was included into the Masjid by ʿAmr ibn Al-ʿĀs despite her reluctance. ʿAmr explained that his action was justified as it would benefit the worshippers who had difficulty performing Ṣalāh in the available space. He also offered her in excess of the value of the property, but she refused the offer. When the matter was brought to the attention of ʿUmar ﷻ, he ordered that the land be returned to her.[2]

Islām teaches justice for all, irrespective of religion, race or language.

1 350 Qissah Wa Qissah Min Qisas as-Sālihīn Wa Nawādir az-Zāhidīn, p64
2 Ṣafhāt Rā'idah Fi Masīratil ʿAdālah, p160

A Lesson in Humility

Abū ʿUthmān al-Ḥiyarī رحمة الله عليه was once invited for a meal by a person who wanted to test his patience. When the saint reached his door, he exclaimed, "I do not have any food at present."

Abū ʿUthmān رحمة الله عليه turned around and left. He had not gone very far when the host called him back. Abū ʿUthmān رحمة الله عليه returned only to be informed that there was no food. In this way, he was led back and forth several times, but he displayed no sign of displeasure. Finally, the man acknowledged, "My teacher, I only intended to test you. What amazing character you have displayed!"

The saint replied, "What you have observed in me is nothing more than what a dog also possesses. When a dog is called, it comes. When it is chased away, it goes."[1]

The hearts of the men of Allāh ﷻ are refined to the extent that they are able to bear trials and hardship with a smile.

بسم الله الرحمن الرحيم

In Pursuit of Knowledge

Imām Aḥmad ibn Ḥanbal رحمة الله عليه was known as a great scholar of his time. One day, a person noticed the Imām holding an ink pot in his hand while proceeding to the lesson of a certain muḥaddith, and asked in surprise, "You are already a scholar of great repute and people regard you as the Imām of the Muslims. What are you going to learn?"

1 Iḥyā' ʿUlūmuddīn, vol 8, p 1465; Qiṣaṣ as-Sālihīn, p96

The learned Imām replied,

مع المحبرة الى المقبرة

"With an ink pot I will go to the graveyard."[1]

A truly knowledgeable person does not regard himself as such, but continues to seek knowledge till death.

بسم الله الرحمن الرحيم

Blessings of a Pious Mother

Khwājah Muʿīnuddīn Chishtī Ajmerī رحمة الله عليه once travelled to Bangladesh. During his journey, seven hundred thousand Hindus accepted Islām at his hands and seven million Muslims made towbah to Allāh and pledged allegiance to him. When he returned home, the signs of joy were clearly visible upon his face.

He kissed his mother and she immediately asked, "My son, why are you so happy?"

He replied, "Mother, Allāh has granted me the good fortune of bringing hundreds of thousands of people into the fold of Islām."

His mother exclaimed, "Son, this is not due to any inherent goodness within you. The credit is due to me."

He asked, "Yes, but please explain what you mean."

She continued, "When you were an infant, I always breast-fed you in the state of wudhū. By the barakah of this, Allāh has granted you the ability to win over the hearts of hundreds of thousands of people to Islām."[2]

---

1 A'immah Arbaaʿh Ke Dilchasp Wāqiʿāt, p284
2 Khawātīne Islām Ke Kārnāme, p30

Virtuous mothers are invaluable assets to society.

بسم الله الرحمن الرحيم

Foresight of a Righteous Mother

Bāyazīd Busṭāmī رحمة الله عليه was a great saint. Junaid Baghdādī رحمة الله عليه while describing his character, said, “Bayazīd’s status amongst the pious servants of Allāh is like the status of Jibra’īl amongst the angels.”

Bāyazīd became an orphan at a tender age. His mother enrolled him at a Madrasah and instructed his teacher, “Do not allow him to come home too often. I fear that his heart would be distracted from the Madrasah if he is allowed to visit home often.”

Accordingly, the teacher kept him at Madrasah for an extended period. One day, the young boy said to his teacher, “I desire to go home for a while.”

His teacher gave him the permission to go home, on condition that he memorised additional lessons while at home.

Bāyazīd arrived home and knocked at the door. His mother was performing wudhū at the time, but recognised the knock to be that of her son. She thought to herself, “If I open the door and allow my son to enter, he will develop the habit of coming home regularly. He will then prefer home and abandon his studies.”

She stepped towards the door and asked, “Who is there?”

The reply came, “Bāyazīd.”

She explained, “I too have a son by the name of Bāyazīd, but I have handed him over for the service of Allāh’s Dīn. Which Bāyazīd are you?”

The young boy was intelligent enough to understand that his mother's desire was that he acquire knowledge. He returned to the Madrasah and continued learning until he completed his studies.[1]

Countless saints, reformers, scholars and soldiers of Allāh ﷻ reached their pinnacles due to the dauntless courage and foresight of their righteous mothers.

بسم الله الرحمن الرحيم

Error of Judgement

Once two students, who were desirous of spiritual reformation, heard about the renowned sage, ʿAbdullāh Ḥanīf رحمة الله عليه, and went to visit him. When they arrived at his spiritual retreat they learnt that he had gone out to see the king. They were surprised and remarked, "He frequents the company of kings! Why did he abandon his life of luxury in the first place?"

With these thoughts they set off for the market place, where they arrived at the shop of a tailor. They entered and requested him to sew one of their torn sleeves. Incidentally, the tailor's scissors suddenly disappeared, and the two were taken to the police. The police chief accused them of the theft and led them off to the king. The king heard the case and passed the judgment for their hands to be cut.

ʿAbdullāh Ḥanīf رحمة الله عليه, who was seated close to the king, witnessed the proceedings. He advised the king, "Set them free as they are not guilty."

The sage then turned to the two students and said, "This should have cleared your doubts. Sometimes I am constrained to visit the king to

1 Khawātīne Islām Ke Kārnāme, p26

handle cases such as yours." The two realised their error of judgment and pledged their allegiance to him.[1]

It is always wise to obtain clarification when in doubt. Premature conclusions and impulsive judgements often serve as a breeding ground for hatred, animosity and unnecessary quarrels.

بسم الله الرحمن الرحيم

An Apt Reply to a Persistent Beggar

A beggar once presented himself at the door of Muʿāwiyah and requested the doorkeeper, "Advise your master that his brother is at his door."

Muʿāwiyah could not visualise the beggar even after the doorkeeper had provided a physical description of him and finally said, "It would be best to usher him in."

When he arrived Muʿāwiyah asked him, "How are you my brother?"

He replied, "I am the son of Ādam and Ḥawwā."

After hearing the reply, Muʿāwiyah instructed his servant to give the beggar a dirham.

The beggar asked, "How can you give only one dirham to your brother?"

Muʿāwiyah explained, "If I were to give something to every single brother of mine, who is from the children of Ādam and Ḥawwā, you would not even receive one dirham."[2]

---

1 Tadhkiratul Awliyā', p253

2 Laṭā'if ʿIlmiyyah, p75

The persistent are often only silenced with an astute reply.

A Unique Reward

Abū Bakr Al-Miskī رحمة الله عليه was asked, "We perpetually smell a fragrance of musk emanating from you. Why is this?"

He replied, "By Allāh, for many years now I have not touched musk. The reason for the fragrance is my encounter with a woman who deceived me into entering her home. She then locked the doors and began to seduce me. I was totally bewildered as there was no way of escape. In desperation I said to her, 'I have a need to purify myself.' She ordered her servant to take me to the bathroom. When I entered, I applied impurity all over my body. I then returned to her. She was appalled to see me in that state and ordered that I be removed from her home. I returned to my home and performed a ghusl. That night, I saw a dream in which I was informed, 'You have performed a unique deed. I will cause your body to emit a beautiful fragrance in this world and the Hereafter.'

When I awoke in the morning, the fragrance of musk continued emanating from my body." The fragrance remained with him until he passed away.[1]

The reward for chastity is indeed sweet.

1 Al-Muwā'iz Wal Majālis, p 224

بسم الله الرحمن الرحيم

Never be Deceived by Tears

Sha'bī narrates: I was once in the company of Qādhī Shuraiḥ when a woman arrived quarrelling with somebody. Soon tears began to flow from her eyes.

I said to the judge, "Do you not see her crying? The decision should be given in her favour as she is the oppressed."

The wise judge replied, "O Sha'bī, the brothers of Yūsuf عليه السلام also came home crying, while they were oppressors and liars. A man should only deliver a judgment based on the truth."[1]

People who deal with conflicts need to be objective and composed in their approach. Emotion and sentimental feelings need to be cast aside as these frequently cloud the path of justice.

بسم الله الرحمن الرحيم

Wisdom of Imām Shāfi'ī رحمة الله عليه

Nabī ﷺ is superior

Baihaqī has narrated that Imām Shāfi'ī رحمة الله عليه said, "Nabī ﷺ was granted what the other prophets were granted, but in a superior form."

Somebody asked, "But 'Īsā عليه السلام was granted the ability to bring the dead back to life."

Imām Shāfi'ī رحمة الله عليه replied, "The crying of a tree trunk is superior to this because giving life to a dry piece of wood is superior to giving life

1 Tafsīr Ar-Rāzī; Laṭā'if 'Ilmiyyah

to a person who had died. And if somebody were to say that Mūsā ﷺ split the ocean we would reply that Nabī ﷺ split the moon. The latter is superior because it is a heavenly miracle, not an earthly one. And if somebody would present the flowing of water from a rock, we would counteract it with the flowing of water from between the fingers of Nabī ﷺ. The latter is superior because water flowing from a rock is an accepted phenomenon, while water flowing from flesh and blood is extraordinary. And if somebody would present to us the miracle of Sulaimān ﷺ, who could control the winds, we would counteract it with the M'irāj."[1]

An easy solution

Imām Shāfi'ī رحمه الله was asked how the following scenario could be explained: "A husband gave his wife a bag which was filled and sealed, saying, 'You are divorced if you do not return the bag to me empty of its contents, but you are not allowed to open it, break it or cut its seal.' "

He replied, "The bag was filled with sugar or salt. If she placed it in water it would dissolve out of the bag and she could then hand it over to him empty."

Wisely clarified

Imām Shāfi'ī رحمه الله was asked how the following scenario could be explained: "A man slaughtered a sheep at his home and then left to complete a task. When he returned home, he said to his wife, "You and the family may eat the sheep, as it is now ḥarām upon me." His wife replied, "The sheep is ḥarām upon us as well."

Imām Shāfi'ī رحمه الله explained, "The man was a disbeliever and had slaughtered the sheep in the name of an idol. While away from home, Allāh had guided him to Islām. When he returned, he said to his wife, "Allāh has granted me the good fortune of accepting Islām and the sheep is therefore ḥarām for me to consume." His family were overjoyed and also accepted Islām. The sheep was now ḥarām upon them as well.[2]

1 Manāqib Al-Imām Ash-Shāfi'ī
2 Manāqib Al-Imām Ash-Shāfi'ī, p81

Knowledge, wisdom and righteousness were the hallmarks of luminaries and scholars throughout Islāmic history.

بسم الله الرحمن الرحيم

Harms of Limited Understanding

Mughīrah Ibn ʿAbdur Raḥmān رحمة الله عليه was a brave warrior who had lost sight from one eye due to an injury sustained in the battles against the Romans during the reign of Maslamah ibn ʿAbdul Malik. He was also very generous by heart and would slaughter a camel and invite people to join in the meal wherever he went. On one occasion, a bedouin arrived, but did not partake of any food. He stared at Mughīrah رحمة الله عليه persistently.

Mughīrah رحمة الله عليه asked, "Are you not going to partake from the food? I see that you are staring at me continuously."

The bedouin replied, "Your food seems pleasant enough, but your eye is doubtful to me."

Mughīrah رحمة الله عليه asked, "What do you doubt regarding my eye?"

He answered, "I see that you have vision from one eye only and that you are feeding people. These are the qualities of Dajjāl!"

Mughīrah رحمة الله عليه explained, "Dajjāl's eyesight will not be harmed due to fighting in the path of Allāh."[1]

Superficial knowledge is dangerous.

1 Tārīkh Dimishq, vol 60, p69

Justice

Sulṭān Malik Shāh was once hunting in a particular area. As he was a distance away from home, he sought residence for the night in a nearby village. The king's men found an ox, slaughtered it and prepared food for the group. The ox belonged to a poor old widow who became very distressed when news reached her, as the ox was the sole source of income for her and her three children. She was even more concerned as she did not have the courage to approach the king or his men.

"Who would listen to the complaint of a poor woman like me?" she thought.

That night, she slept uneasily, but the next morning, she made up her mind to approach the king. "Allāh has entrusted him with our affairs and he should provide protection for the weak amongst us," she assured herself. She made an attempt to reach the king, but was unsuccessful.

Incidentally, she received information that the king would soon cross the famous bridge of Isfahān. She proceeded to the bridge and remained there awaiting the king's arrival. As he passed by, she courageously asked, "O son of Alp Arsalān, will you meet out justice to me on this bridge or on the Bridge of Ṣirāṭ? Choose whichever pleases you."

The king was astonished by the amazing question. He jumped down from his horse and asked, "I do not have the strength to account on the Bridge of Ṣirāṭ. I prefer to meet out justice here and now. Please tell me what your complaint is."

The old woman narrated her story and the king expressed his dislike at his men's unacceptable conduct. As compensation for her ox, he ordered that she be given seventy oxen. Only after she expressed her pleasure over his decision, did he mount his horse and continue on his journey.[1]

1 Khawātine Islām Ke Īmān Afroz Wāqiʿāt, p 269

Those who are Allāh-conscious prefer to promptly rectify their wrongs in this world because they fully realise the gravity of accountability in the Hereafter.

بسم الله الرحمن الرحيم

Overlooking a Wife's Mistake

There was once a poor man whose meager income could only provide his family with the most basic of meals. For six months at a time, they would consume only dhāl. One day, he managed to purchase some chicken and handed it over to his wife to prepare. He was excited over the idea of tasting meat after months of simple food. When the meal was served, he immediately realised that it contained too much salt. But, he kept his composure and ate without uttering a word. He thought to himself, "O Allāh, had my own daughter added too much salt to a meal, I would have liked my son-in-law to forgive her mistake and not say a word of rebuke to her. My wife is also the daughter of somebody. She too has parents who would like her mistakes to be overlooked. Over and above that, she is Your slave and I forgive her mistake for Your pleasure."

After he passed away, a pious man saw him in a dream and asked, "How did you fare?"

He replied, "Allāh informed me of all my sins and I was convinced that I would be cast into Jahannam. But, Allāh said to me: 'Go, I have forgiven you because you forgave one mistake of my slave. You did not strike, scold or abuse her when she added too much salt to the food. I forgive you because you forgave her.' "[1]

1 Bikhre Motī, p321

Marriage partners who overlook each others mistakes live happier lives and are divinely rewarded in the Hereafter for their patience.

An Honoured Guest

Once Imām Shāfi'ī رحمة الله عليه travelled to Madīnah to visit and learn from Imām Mālik رحمة الله عليه. After completing his Ṣalāh, he noticed a group of students seated around a man with a turban who was seated on an elevated platform and narrating Aḥādīth. He assumed that this was Imām Mālik رحمة الله عليه and sat down amongst the students. Imām Mālik رحمة الله عليه was at the time narrating the Aḥādīth from his famous Muwaṭṭā.

Imām Shāfi'ī رحمة الله عليه explains, "I picked up a blade of grass, moistened it with saliva from my mouth and began to write the Aḥādīth on my palm. As the other students were all writing with pen and paper, Imām Mālik رحمة الله عليه noticed my unusual behaviour. The Imām narrated a hundred and twenty-six Aḥādīth before he stopped for Ṣalāh. As the students dispersed, Imām Mālik رحمة الله عليه called me and asked, "It appears as if you are a stranger here."

"Yes, I have come from Makkah," I replied.

"What were you doing on your palm?" he asked.

"I was writing the Aḥādīth you were dictating," I replied.

"Show me what you have written," he instructed, and I showed him my palm.

"There is nothing written here," he remarked.

"I did not have a pen or any paper, hence I decided to record the Aḥādīth as best I could," I explained.

Imām Mālik رحمة الله عليه was disappointed and said to me, "This is contrary to the dictates of respect which Aḥādīth demand."

"I only wrote the Aḥādīth on my palm as an outward gesture. In reality, I have memorised each Ḥadīth," I explained.

"In that case, please narrate some of the Aḥādīth I dictated," he requested. I immediately narrated the hundred and twenty-six Aḥādīth with the chain of narrators and text as I had heard them from him."

Imām Mālik رحمة الله عليه was impressed and said, "Young man, please accept my invitation and be my guest for tonight." I readily agreed. He returned home and advised his daughters about my coming. They were virtuous and knowledgeable young women, who would also attend the lessons of their father. Sitting behind a veil, they would even correct the mistakes of other reciters by striking together sticks in a particular manner.

When they heard about the arrival of a scholar that night, they prepared a meal, arranged the bedding and muṣallā (prayer-mat) and placed sufficient water for their guest. That night, Imām Shāfi'ī رحمة الله عليه ate to his fill. The next morning, he left with Imām Mālik رحمة الله عليه to perform Fajr.

After Ishrāq, they returned home and Imām Mālik رحمة الله عليه asked Imām Shāfi'ī رحمة الله عليه, "My daughters have some doubts about you. They thought that you were a pious man, according to what I had informed them, but their experience has been quite different. Firstly, the food they had prepared would have been sufficient for a number of people, but you consumed it all single-handedly! There was no need to even wash the utensils. Secondly, they placed a muṣallā for you to perform optional Ṣalāh at night, but they found that it had not been utilised at all. The water that they had placed for you was also not used. It appears as if you did not perform tahajjud Ṣalāh, nor did you perform wudhū before proceeding to the Masjid to perform Fajr. They have found your behaviour quite ambiguous."

Imām Shāfi'ī رحمة الله عليه explained, "Your food contained so much of nūr (celestial beauty) that I could feel it filling my bosom with every morsel I placed into my mouth. I thought that I would never have the opportunity of consuming such blessed food again, and decided to eat as much of it as I could. When I lay down to rest, the food that I had consumed, gave me the spiritual strength to remain awake. I began pondering over Aḥādīth. The Ḥadīth which was foremost in my mind was when Nabī ﷺ lovingly said to the young boy whose pet bird had died,

يا أبا عمير ما فعل النغير؟

O Abū ʿUmair, what has happened to Nughair?

From this Ḥadīth I extracted forty fiqhī masāil (laws). I thought about how a title should be chosen, how young children should be addressed and how the distressed should be consoled. As I had remained in the state of wudhū throughout the night, there was no need to perform wudhū for Fajr Ṣalāh.[1]

The private lives of the pious are an embodiment of spiritual dedication.

بسم الله الرحمن الرحيم

Zeal for Knowledge

ʿAbdullāh ibn ʿAbbās ؓ narrates: After the demise of Nabī ﷺ, I said to a young Ṣaḥābī from the Anṣār, "Come, let us proceed to the Ṣaḥābah as there are still many of them around."

He said to me, "You surprise me, O Ibn ʿAbbās! Do you really think that people will approach you to answer their questions when they have other great Ṣaḥābah amongst them?"

I left him and proceeded to learn from the Ṣaḥābah. If I got to know of any particular Ṣaḥābī who had narrated a Ḥadīth, I would go to him. Sometimes, he would be lying down for a nap. I would spread my shawl at his doorstep, while the wind would blow dust into my face. When he would awake and come out, he would notice me and say, "O cousin of Nabī ﷺ, why did you come to me? If you had sent a message I would have come to you!"

1 Bikhre Motī, p440

I would reply, "No, you are more worthy of my coming to you." I would then enquire about the Ḥadīth I had come to learn. After some time, the Ṣaḥābī from the Anṣār noticed many people around me seeking answers to their questions from me and remarked, "This young man was more intelligent than me."[1]

True knowledge is acquired when a student humbles himself.

بسم الله الرحمن الرحيم

Legacy of Books and Reading

Moulānā Abul Ḥasan ʿAlī Nadwī رحمة الله عليه narrates: Our home was one of scholars and authors. My father was one of the great writers of his time. Just as family traditions pass from generation to generation, so too did the love for books and learning pass on from my grandparents and parents and inspire my sisters and myself. The love for books was almost like an addiction within us. We would read whatever we could and would purchase books with any money we obtained.

One day, one or two ānās[2] came into my possession somehow. I was very young and was not even aware that only bookshops sell books. I went to Amīnābād and entered a pharmacy where I presented my little money and asked for a book. The worker probably regarded me as a simple young boy who did not know that pharmacies do not sell books. He gave me a book which had a listing of medications and returned my money. I was absolutely delighted to have received a book and my money back. I returned home and joyously placed it in my little library which I had made from the books that had been discarded by my father.[3]

---

1 Al-Bidāyah Wan Nihāyah vol 12, p86

2 Indian currency.

3 Baro Ka Bachpan, p154

Children follow in their parents' footsteps.

~

Cultured parents inculcate the noble qualities of reading and scholarship within their children, while the unwise deny themselves and their children the opportunity of benefiting from the books and archives of knowledge.

بسم الله الرحمن الرحيم

Punishment for Slander

It is narrated that a woman passed away in the outlying areas of Madīnah and a group of women gathered to perform her ghusl. As the hand of the woman who was washing her body passed over the thigh of the deceased woman, she remarked, "Sisters! This woman had an illicit relationship with so-and-so man."

The moment these words left her lips, her hand became fixed to the thigh of the deceased woman. As hard as she tried, her hand would not separate. Time began to pass, and the family of the deceased urged her to hurry along as night was approaching and they still had to perform the Janāzah Ṣalāh and burial.

She replied, "I am trying to release my hand, but I am unable to do so."

The night passed and the next day dawned, but her hand remained firmly attached. The family decided to approach the ʿUlamā' for guidance.

"Cut her hand," one of the scholars advised.

But, the woman's family did not accept the ruling, saying, "We will not allow her to bear the difficulty of having a hand cut."

They approached another scholar who advised, "Take a knife and cut the flesh from the thigh of the deceased."

But, this time the deceased's family refused the advice, saying, "We do not want to disfigure her body."

Three days passed without any resolution in sight. The heat was intense and the body began to produce a stench. News quickly spread to various surrounding towns and villages. After much deliberation, they decided to take the matter to Imām Mālik رحمة الله عليه, who was then the chief judge of Madīnah. When they explained the case to Imām Mālik رحمة الله عليه, he replied, "Lead me to the scene."

From behind a veil, he asked the woman who had given the ghusl, "Sister, did you perhaps utter any words at the time when your hand became fixed to the deceased's body?"

She replied, "All I said was that the deceased woman had an illicit relationship with so-and-so man."

Imām Mālik رحمة الله عليه continued, "Do you have four eye-witnesses for the accusation you levelled?"

"No," she answered.

Imām Mālik رحمة الله عليه then asked, "Did the deceased woman personally inform you of the sin you are accusing her of?"

"No," she answered.

Imām Mālik رحمة الله عليه asked, "Then why did you make such an allegation?"

"I said so because I saw her passing through the door of the house of this particular man," she explained.

Imām Mālik رحمة الله عليه then recited the verse of the Qur'ān:

وَالَّذِينَ يَرْمُونَ الْمُحْصَنَاتِ ثُمَّ لَمْ يَأْتُوا بِأَرْبَعَةِ شُهَدَاءَ فَاجْلِدُوهُمْ ثَمَانِينَ جَلْدَةً وَلَا
تَقْبَلُوا لَهُمْ شَهَادَةً أَبَدًا وَأُولَئِكَ هُمُ الْفَاسِقُونَ

And those who accuse chaste women, and then do not produce four witnesses, flog them with eighty lashes, and reject their testimony forever. And these are indeed the transgressors.
(Sūrah Nūr, Verse 4)

He explained, "You accused a deceased woman despite having no witnesses. As chief judge, I suggest that she be given eighty lashes."

After eighty lashes had been given, her hand separated from the deceased's body without any effort.[1]

Islām grants exceptional honour and protection to women by inflicting a severe punishment upon those who choose to accuse them without conclusive evidence.

بسم الله الرحمن الرحيم

Wisely Apprehended

One day, Khalīf Manṣūr was seated on an elevated platform overlooking the city when he noticed a person walking despondently from one street to another. He instructed a servant to summon the man and, when he arrived, he asked what the problem was.

The man explained, "I travelled on business and, after some time, returned home with a substantial profit. I presented the money to my wife, who informed me that our home had been burgled and all our possessions were stolen. She further explained that there was no sign of any forced entry through the walls or the roof.

Khalīf Manṣūr asked, "How long have you been married to your wife?"

"One year," he replied.

"Was she previously married?" he enquired.

"Yes," he answered.

"Did she have any children from her previous marriage?"

"No," he replied.

1 Bikhre Motī, p66

"Is she young or old?" he enquired further.

"She is young," was the answer.

Khalīf Manṣūr then instructed that a particular bottle of ʿiṭr (scent) be brought to him. It had a unique fragrance and was only used by the Khalīf. He handed the bottle to the man and advised, "Use this ʿiṭr. It will assist in removing your sorrow."

After the man left, the Khalīf summoned four of his most trusted security guards and instructed them to smell the ʿiṭr. He continued, "Proceed to each of the doors of the city and bring to me any such person upon whom you smell this fragrance."

In the meanwhile, the man returned home and handed the bottle to his wife, saying, "The Khalīf has given this to me." She smelt it and after some time called for her paramour. She advised him to apply the ʿiṭr and also secretly handed him some money. The man applied the ʿiṭr and left. As he passed one of the doors of the city, the guard on duty smelt the fragrance and apprehended him. He was immediately brought to the Khalīf.

Khalīf Manṣūr asked, "From where did you acquire such a unique fragrance?"

He answered, "I purchased it."

"From where?" The Khalīf asked.

The man panicked and began making excuses.

Khalīf Manṣūr summoned his chief of police and instructed, "Arrest him and keep him in confinement. If he returns the money he has stolen, you may release him. If he does not return it, whip him a thousand lashes."

After the two had left, he again summoned the police chief and explained, "Confine him and frighten him a bit, but do not lash him until I instruct you to do so."

Accordingly, the man was kept in solitary confinement. After a short while, he confessed to the theft of the money and brought it to the police chief. When Khalīf Manṣūr was informed, he called for the owner and asked, "If your entire wealth is returned to you, will you grant me the choice of handling the matter between you and your wife?"

"Yes, I will," he replied.

Khalīf Manṣūr said, "Here is your wealth and I hereby annul your marriage to your wife."[1]

Criminals are often apprehended and disgraced by a bit of insight and wisdom.

بسم الله الرحمن الرحيم

A Loaf of Bread

When Abū Mūsā Al-Ashaʿrī ﷺ was on his death-bed, he called his children and advised them, "Remember the man with a loaf of bread."

He continued, "Once, there was a pious monk who had dedicated himself to the worship of Allāh for seventy years, and only left his monastery for one day. Unfortunately, Shaiṭān succeeded in tempting him towards a beautiful woman, and he spent seven days and nights with her. He then realised his error and left her, repenting to Allāh ﷻ. With every step he took he prayed and prostrated to Allāh ﷻ. One night, he sought refuge close to a shop where there were twelve destitute men. He was utterly exhausted and laid down amongst them. It so happened that a monk in the town would send twelve loaves of bread to these men each night. That night, the servant arrived with the bread and began distributing one to each person. When he reached the repentant man, he considered him to be one of the destitute men and handed him a loaf as well.

After he had completed, the one who did not receive his loaf called out, "Why did you not give me a loaf tonight?"

The servant replied, "Do you think I have ignored you? Go on, ask whether I have accidentally given any of your companions two loaves."

1 Laṭā'if ʿIlmiyyah, p87

But, they all replied that none of them had received more than one.

Angrily, the servant said to him, "By Allāh, I will not give you anything tonight?"

The repentant man realised what had happened and handed the loaf he had been given over to the man who did not receive his share for the night. That night, he passed away. His seventy years of worship were weighed, but the seven nights he had spent in sin with the woman outweighed his worship. His noble act of giving the loaf of bread away at night was weighed and this tilted the pan in his favour."

Abū Mūsā ended with the words, "My beloved children, remember the man with the loaf of bread."[1]

To endure difficulties for the comfort of others is a noble virtue.

Secret to Success

Amīr Dost Muḥammad Khān, the governor of Kabul, was attacked by a foreign king and his army. As the news reached him, he sent out an army headed by his son to repel the enemy. Soon, a second message reached him that his son's army had been defeated. The report also mentioned that his son was now fleeing from the battlefield and was being pursued by the enemy. Amīr Dost Muḥammad was shocked. The defeat of his army, the disgraceful condition of his son and the humiliation of his people were too much for him to bear. He entered his home devastated and narrated the tragic report to his wife.

His wife immediately replied, "The report you have received is false."

1 Kitābut Tawwābīn, p 97

He asked, bewildered, "How can it be false? It has come to us through my special intelligence agents."

But she resolutely answered, "He can never be defeated in this way."

The leader thought to himself, "She is a woman and will stubbornly insist that her opinion is correct." But the very next day, the news arrived that the previous report was indeed false and that the army was returning triumphantly.

Amīr Dost Muḥammad Khān returned home and related the news to his wife, who expressed her gratitude to Allāh ﷻ for the safety of her son. He asked her, "But how did you know that he could not be defeated? What led you to refute the report of my entire government intelligence network?"

She replied, "Nothing much. Allāh ﷻ protected my honour. It is my secret and I do not wish to divulge it."

But, her husband insisted, and she finally agreed to explain, "From the very inception of my pregnancy, I took an oath that I would never consume doubtful food as I knew that ḥalāl food produces good character, whereas ḥarām food produces bad character. I continued my habit of abstaining from doubtful food even after he was born so that my milk would not impact negatively upon his character. In addition, I would only breastfeed him in the state of wudhū and after performing two rakāts of Nafl Ṣalāh. For this reason, I am convinced that his character would never be immoral. He could pass away in the battlefield as a martyr as this constitutes good character, but he could never flee from the battlefield as this is sinful. Hence, I was able to convincingly challenge the news of your entire army and government intelligence network."[1]

Righteous mothers abstain from doubtful food and perform optional meritorious deeds which contribute to the spiritual excellence of their offspring.

1 Khawātīne Islām Ke Kārnāme, p144

Adopting the Principles of the Righteous

A person, who had the habit of disguising himself in various forms, would frequent the court of the ruler ʿĀlamgīr Aurangzeb رحمة الله عليه in order to receive a reward from him. The ruler was wise and experienced and would always recognise him, saying, "You are so-and-so. I have recognised you." The man would leave and reappear after a few days in another guise, only to be identified again. After being unsuccessful many times, he decided to stay away from the court for some time.

After a year had passed, news spread in the city that a very pious saint had come and was in seclusion at the top of a mountain outside the city. If one succeeded in speaking to or even greeting him, it would be regarded as a moment of great fortune, as the sage spent almost all of his time in solitude. It was thought that he was a student of Mujaddid Alfe Thānī رحمة الله عليه and a dedicated follower of the Sunnah.

ʿĀlamgīr Aurangzeb رحمة الله عليه also heard about the saint but did not pay much attention to him. His ministers advised him several times to meet the pious man, but the ruler declined each time. Eventually, they convinced him to visit the sage and request his duā's.

"If he is indeed a pious saint of Allāh, the visit will be beneficial for us," he said as they left for the mountain.

When they arrived, the ruler sat down respectfully. He asked for duʿās and presented a gift to the sage, who refused to accept it. As the ruler was on his way back, the sage called out, "Did you not recognise me? I am the man who used to come to your court disguised, but you always recognised me."

The ruler admitted, "Fine, you got the better of me finally, but tell me one thing. Why did you refuse the large sum of money I presented to you? You have after all been trying to earn some reward from me by disguising yourself all this time."

The man replied, "This is not the conduct of the sages. When I disguised myself as one of them and adopted their ways, I felt embarrassed to accept a gift from a ruler, in accordance with their principles. For this reason I did not accept your gift."[1]

A man who mimicked the sages was wise enough to adopt their principles. Those who claim to follow the prophets and sages should similarly adopt their teachings, principles and conduct, else such claims are little more than lip service.

بِسْمِ اللّٰهِ الرَّحْمٰنِ الرَّحِيْمِ

The Thief Who Fasted

Abū Bakr Ash-Shiblī narrates: Once I was travelling to Syria with a group of travellers when we were attacked by a gang of bedouin thieves. They robbed us of our possessions and presented them to their leader. Amongst the goods, was a bag of sugar and almonds. The thieves began to eat them but their leader refrained.

I noticed this and asked him, "Why are you not eating?"

He replied, "I am fasting."

I remarked in astonishment, "You are a highway robber, you steal from people and commit murder, yet you claim to be fasting!"

He replied, "O Shaikh, I do so in order to keep open the doors of reconciliation."

After sometime, I saw the same gang leader in the state of "iḥrām", performing Ṭawāf of the Ka'bah.

I asked in astonishment, "Are you the same man?"

He answered, "Yes. That very same fast is the reason for me being here."[2]

1 Bikhre Motī, p 494

2 Kitābut Tawwābīn p 278

A person should never allow his sins to deter him from performing good deeds. Often, Shaiṭān discourages a person from doing good deeds by creating feelings of despondency. One should persevere with the obligatory and optional acts of worship, with the intention that these will eventually pave the way for him to abstain from sin.

بسم الله الرحمن الرحيم

Dealing with Hearts

Aṣmaʿī narrates: I was once walking through a village, when I came across a stone upon which a couplet had been written,

أيا معشر العشاق بالله خبروا

اذا حل عشق بالفتى كيف يصنع

O lovers! By Allāh, inform me!
If a young man is overpowered by love, what should he do?

So I wrote underneath it,

يداوي هواه ثم يكتم سره

ويخشع في كل الامور ويخضع

He should treat his desire, then conceal his secret
And he should humble himself in all matters and submit (before Allāh)

I returned the next day, and found another couplet written beneath mine,

فكيف يداوي والهوى قاتل الفتى

وفي كل يوم قلبه يتقطع

But how can it be treated when that desire fights the young man
And every day his heart is shattered into pieces?

So I wrote beneath it,

إذا لم يجد صبرا لكتمان سره

فليس له شيء سوى الموت أنفع

If he cannot be patient to conceal his secret
Then nothing except death can benefit him!

I then returned on the third day and found a young man lying dead at the stone. I said, "*Lā ḥawlā wa lā quwwata illā billāhil ʿAliyil ʿAẓīm!*"
Prior to his death he had written,

سمعنا و أطعنا ثم متنا فبلغوا

سلامي على من كان للوصل يمنع

هنيئا لارباب النعيم نعيمهم

و للعاشق المسكين ما يتجرعوا

We have heard and we have obeyed; now we are dead so proclaim
my greetings to the one who prevented me from attaining my objective.
Compliments to the possessors of bliss for attaining their happiness;
And the poor lover has earned what they led him to accept.[1]

1 Al-Mustaṭraf Fi Kulli Fannim Mustaẓraf, vol 2, p170

Be soft when interacting with people as you are dealing with hearts and not stones.

Evidence from the Book of Allāh

Rabʿī narrates: We were with Imām Shāfiʿī one day, when an old man dressed in a woolen garment came to us with a walking-stick in his hand. Imām Shāfiʿī stood up, neatened his clothing and after greeting the old man, sat down again. The Imām then continued gazing at him respectfully. The old man then said, "May I ask a question?"

Imām Shāfiʿī replied, "Yes, you may."

The old man asked, "What is the ḥujjah (proof) in the religion of Allāh?"

Imām Shāfiʿī replied, "The Book of Allāh."

The old man then asked, "And what else?"

Imām Shāfiʿī answered, "The Sunnah of Nabī."

The old man continued, "What else?"

Imām Shāfiʿī replied, "The consensus of the Ummah."

The old man enquired, "What is your proof for saying 'consensus of the Ummah'?"

Imām Shāfiʿī pondered for a while and the old man said, "I will give you three days' grace. You either produce the evidence from the Book of Allāh or else you should repent to Allāh."

Imām Shāfiʿī's face changed colour and he then left us. He returned on the third day, between Ẓuhr and ʿAṣr Ṣalāh. His face, hands and legs were swollen and he was visibly ill. He sat down, and after a few moments, the old man arrived. He greeted, sat down and then said, "Did you find the answer to my question?"

Imām Shāfiʿī replied, "Yes,

وَمَن يُشَاقِقِ الرَّسُولَ مِن بَعْدِ مَا تَبَيَّنَ لَهُ الْهُدَىٰ وَيَتَّبِعْ غَيْرَ سَبِيلِ الْمُؤْمِنِينَ نُوَلِّهِ مَا
تَوَلَّىٰ وَنُصْلِهِ جَهَنَّمَ وَسَاءَتْ مَصِيرًا

"And whoever opposes the Rasūl after the guidance has been made clear to him, and follows a path other than that of the believers, We will keep him on the path he has chosen, and burn him in Hell. And what an evil destination." (Sūrah An-Nisā', 115)

Allāh ﷻ would certainly not burn a person in Hell for opposing the believers unless it was compulsory to follow them."

The old man exclaimed, "You have spoken the truth." He then stood up and left.

Imām Shāfiʿī رحمه الله then said to those around him, "I read the Qur'an thrice daily for the last three days until I found this verse."[1]

The Imāms of fiqh invariably based their rulings upon solid evidence obtained from the authentic sources of Islām. May Allāh ﷻ reward them for sacrificing their health and time in order to search for answers to the intricate matters of faith.

بسم الله الرحمن الرحيم

Repayment for a Generous Gesture

A Shaikh (spiritual leader), one day, set out to meet a group of his companions. They were forty in number and all of them had spent the last three days without any food. When he heard this, he advised them,

1 Siyar Aaʿlām An-Nubalā, vol 10, p84

"Allāh has allowed his servants to utilise means in order to achieve things. Allāh mentions :

فَامْشُوا فِي مَنَاكِبِهَا وَكُلُوا مِن رِّزْقِهِ

"And walk in the paths (of the earth) and consume His sustenance."
(Sūrah Mulk, verse 15)

Let us, therefore, decide who amongst us will venture out and bring us something to eat."

They chose one of the disciples who proceeded to the outskirts of Baghdād. Unfortunately, he could not find anybody to assist him, and hunger and tiredness overpowered him. He sat down close to the door of a Christian doctor, whose consulting room was crowded with patients.

The doctor prescribed for each of them a particular medicine and then turned to the hungry disciple and asked, "What ailment do you have?"

The disciple did not find it appropriate to disclose his condition to the doctor and decided to extend his hand for the doctor to make a diagnosis.

The doctor felt it and remarked, "I know the cure for this ailment," and instructed his servant, "Go to the market and bring me one raṭl[1] each of rice, roast and sweetmeats."

The disciple remarked, "This ailment afflicts forty of my companions also!"

In response, the doctor said, "In that case, fetch forty raṭls of each."

When the servant returned with the food, the doctor handed it over to the disciple and said to him, "Take this to your companions."

The disciple then left, together with a porter, carrying the goods and headed off for Duwairah. The doctor quietly followed them to ascertain whether the disciple had spoken the truth. When they arrived, the doctor concealed himself outside and the disciple entered. He placed the food before the Shaikh and the other disciples. The Shaikh refused to eat the food and asked, "My disciple, how did you acquire this food?"

---

1 A measurement of weight.

The disciple recounted the full story and the Shaikh said, "Do you all feel happy to consume the food which a Christian has sent to you, without any recompense?"

They asked, "But, how do we recompense him?"

The Shaikh explained, "Before partaking of the food, make du'ā' to Allāh that Allāh saves him from the Fire (by guiding him)." They all made du'ā', not realising that he was outside listening to them.

When the doctor noticed them abstaining from the food despite their hunger, and he heard the words of the Shaikh, he knocked at the door. When it was opened, he stepped in, cut his Zunnār (the customary Christian cloth which is worn around the waist) and exclaimed, "I bear witness that there is no deity worthy of worship besides Allāh and I bear witness that Muḥammad is the prophet of Allāh."[1]

Allāh ﷻ has created the world as an abode of means and these need to be employed to acquire food and other necessities of life.

~

Muslims should endeavour to repay the kindness of others by making du'ā' for their guidance and well-being.

بسم الله الرحمن الرحيم

Abstaining from Temptation

During the time of 'Umar ibn Khaṭṭāb ؓ, there was a youth who was exceptional in terms of his spirituality and piety. He would frequent the Masjid and listen intently to the Ḥadīth narrated by the Ṣaḥābah ؓ. Umar

1 Kitābut Tawwābīn, p 304

ؓ too admired his dedication. He had an elderly father, and every night after performing Īshā', the young man would visit him. On his way, he would pass by the door of a woman who became infatuated with him.

One night, as he was walking by, she began to entice him until he finally succumbed and followed her. As they entered her home, he recalled a verse of the Qur'ān,

إِنَّ الَّذِينَ اتَّقَوْاْ إِذَا مَسَّهُمْ طَائِفٌ مِّنَ الشَّيْطَانِ تَذَكَّرُواْ فَإِذَا هُم مُّبْصِرُونَ

Verily, those who are the pious, when an evil thought comes to them from Shaiṭān, they remember (Allāh), and they then see (the guidance). (Sūrah Al-Aa'rāf, verse 201)

He immediately fell to the ground unconscious and had to be carried to the home of his father. He remained in that state until a third of the night had passed. When he opened his eyes, his father asked him what had happened, and he related what had transpired.

His father asked, "My dear son, which verse did you recite?"

The youth recited it and fell unconscious a second time. This time his family and neighbours tried to revive him but it was in vain. He had already passed away. They performed his ghusl, dressed him in a burial shroud and buried him that same night. The next morning, the news reached 'Umar ؓ who went and consoled his father. He then went to his grave and recited,

وَلِمَنْ خَافَ مَقَامَ رَبِّهِ جَنَّتَانِ

But for him who fears the standing before his Allah, there will be two Gardens (in Paradise). (Sūrah Ar-Raḥmān, verse 46)

From the grave the young man replied, "Allah has already granted this to me twice in Jannah."[1]

1 Tārīkh Dimishq, vol 45, p 450; Al Bidāyah Wan Nihāyah

Allāh handsomely rewards a person who abstains from Ḥarām.

بسم الله الرحمن الرحيم

A Wise Choice of a Marriage Partner

Yaḥyā ibn Yaḥyā An-Naysābūrī narrates: I was with Sufyān ibn ʿUyaynah, when a man approached him and said, "O Abū Muḥammad, I have come to complain to you about my wife. I am the most disgraced and dishonoured of entities to her."

Sufyān lowered his head in silence for a while, and then raising it, asked, "Were you perhaps inclined to her so that the union would increase your honour?"

The man replied, "Yes, Abū Muḥammad."

Sufyān then said, "A person who seeks honour will be tested with disgrace. A person who seeks wealth will be tested with poverty. But, a person who seeks dīn (spirituality), Allāh will grant him both honour and wealth together with spirituality."

He then narrated to him a story, "We were four brothers: Muḥammad, ʿImrān, Ibrāhīm and I. Muḥammad was the eldest, ʿImrān was the youngest and I was in between them in age. When Muḥammad intended to marry, he was inclined to lineage and married a woman of better lineage than himself. But, Allāh tested him with disgrace. ʿImrān was inclined to wealth, so he married a woman who was wealthier than him. But, Allāh tested him with poverty. They took all his wealth and did not return anything to him. So, I pondered over their choices. When Maʿmar ibn Rāshid came to visit us, I consulted with him by narrating to him the stories of my brothers. He reminded me of the Aḥādīth narrated by ʿĀ'ishah and Yaḥyā ibn Jaʿdah. As for the Ḥadīth narrated by Jaʿdah, Nabī said,

" تنكح المرأة على أربع: دينها، وحسبها، ومالها، وجمالها، فعليك بذات الدين تربت يداك

"A woman is married for four reasons: spirituality, lineage, wealth and beauty. Marry one with spirituality and you will be successful."

As for the Ḥadīth narrated by ʿĀ'ishah رضي الله عنها, Nabī ﷺ said,

أعظم النساء بركة أيسرهن مؤنة

"The woman with the greatest blessings is the one with the least Mahr."

So I chose spirituality and a small Mahr, in conformity with the Sunnah of Nabī ﷺ. The result was that Allāh granted me honour and wealth together with spirituality."[1]

One of the greatest bounties a husband can possess is the company of a righteous wife.

بسم الله الرحمن الرحيم

A Man of Integrity

A group of men, who had allegedly rebelled against Ḥajjāj, were brought before him. He commanded that they be beheaded. When they reached the last man, the time for Maghrib Ṣalāh entered and Ḥajjāj instructed Qutaibah ibn Muslim , "Take him with you for the night and bring him to me early tomorrow morning."

1 Tahdhībul Kamāl Mizzi, vol 11, p 194

Qutaibah continues, "I left with the man. As we walked along, he said to me, "Will you be kind to me?"

"How?" I asked.

"I have neither rebelled against the Muslims, nor would I like to fight them. Unfortunately, I have been falsely accused. I have in my possession wealth and other goods which people have left in trust with me. Will you be kind enough to allow me to return to my home, so that I can return these trusts and give parting advice to my family? I give you my guarantee that I will return," he pleaded.

I was amazed at his request and could not suppress my laughter. After walking a little further, he repeated his request, "I take an oath in Allah's Name that I will return to you."

I could not hold back, and submitted, "Go!" The moment he was out of sight, I said to myself, "What have you done?"

I returned home, worried and perturbed. My family inquired regarding my sad state of mind and I informed them what had transpired. They warned, "You certainly have the courage to oppose Ḥajjāj!" I passed the night in worry and anxiety. At the time of the Fajr Adhān, there was a knock at the door, and I opened it. To my amazement, there stood the man.

I exclaimed, "You have returned?"

He replied, "*Subḥānallāh*! I took an oath in the Name of Allāh to return to you. Did you expect me to break my promise and escape from you?"

I explained, "I will do whatever is in my ability to assist you." We arrived at the door of Ḥajjāj and sat down awaiting his arrival.

When I entered, he said to me, "Qutaibah, where is your prisoner?"

I replied, "He is at the door, Amīrul Mu'minīn, but I have an amazing incident to relate to you regarding him."

He asked, "What is it?"

After I had recounted the night's proceedings, he requested the prisoner to enter. He then turned to me and asked, "Qutaibah, would you like me to hand him over to you?"

"Yes!" I exclaimed.

"Then take him along with you," he said. I then led him away with me.

As we left the court, I said to him, "You are free to go."

The man looked up at the heavens and remarked, "All praise be to You, my Lord." Without a word of appreciation or even a greeting, he left.

I thought to myself, "This is surely an insane person!"

After three days, he returned once again and said, "May Allāh reward you well. I did not forget your kindness upon me, however I disliked associating partners with Allāh when I praised Him."[1]

A Muslim's word is his honour.

بسم الله الرحمن الرحيم

Astounding Memory

Abū Zurʿah was a great muḥaddith who used to narrate Aḥādīth to many students. One particular student, who frequented his lessons, was newly married. One day, the lesson was prolonged and the student reached home late. His wife was angry, and as he entered, she asked, "I was anxiously waiting for you. Why are you late?"

The student replied, "I was certainly not wasting my time. I was in the lesson of my teacher, Abū Zurʿah."

Furiously, she exclaimed, "Your teacher knows nothing, how do you expect to learn anything!"

Now the young man also lost his temper and remarked, "If my teacher cannot recite a hundred thousand Aḥādīth from memory then I issue you three divorces!" The next morning, his anger subsided and he realised the gravity of his statement. "How foolish was I to make such a remark," he thought to himself.

1 Min Qaṣaṣil ʿArab, vol 3, p34

His wife asked, "Since my divorce is conditional upon your teacher's memory, please advise whether I am separated from you or not."

"Only my teacher will be able to advise regarding this," he replied and left. He arrived at the door of Abū Zurʿah and explained what had transpired the night before. "Is my nikāḥ (marriage) intact or has the divorce taken place?" he asked anxiously.

The muḥaddith smiled and replied, "You may return to your wife, rest assured that your marriage is still intact. I can recite a hundred thousand Aḥādīth from memory in the same way as people can recite Sūrah Fātiḥah."[1]

Couples need to discuss contentious issues without anger and emotion.

~

Islāmic history is replete with men who utilised their potential and capabilities in the service of the faith.

This compilation of short stories has been completed by the grace and mercy of Allāh ﷻ. All praise belongs to Allāh ﷻ and peace and salutations be upon our beloved Nabī ﷺ.

1 Bikhre Motī, p840

Bibliography

TAFĀSĪR

Ar-Rāzi, Muḥammad ibn Amar ibn al-Ḥusain Fakhruddīn. *Tafsīr Al-Fakhr Ar-Rāzī.* Beirūt: Dārul Fikr, 1401 / 1981

Ibn Kathīr, Ismā'īl ibn 'Umar Al-Qurashī Al-Dimashqī. *Tafsīr Ibn Kathīr*. Jīzah: Maktabah Awlādush Shaikh Lit Turāth, undated

AḤĀDĪTH

Al-'Asqalānī, Ibn Ḥajar. *Fatḥul Bārī.* Beirut: Dārul Ma'rifah, 1390

TĀRĪKH AND ASMĀ UR-RIJĀL

Adh-Dhahabī, Shamsuddīn Abū 'Abdullāh Muḥammad ibn Aḥmad ibn 'Uthmān ibn Qāimāz ibn 'Abdullāh. *Siyar Aa'lām An Nubalā'*. Beirūt: Muassasatur Risālah, 1417/1996

Adh-Dhahabī, Shamsuddīn Abū 'Abdullāh Muḥammad ibn Aḥmad ibn 'Uthmān ibn Qāimāz ibn 'Abdullāh. *Tadhkiratul Ḥuffāẓ.* Hyderabād Deccan: Dā'iratul Ma'ārif Al-'Uthmāniyyah, 1375/1953

Al-Mizzī, Jamāluddīn Abī Al-Ḥajjāj Yūsuf. *Tahdhībul Kamāl Fī Asmā'ir Rijāl.* Beirūt: Mu'assasatur Risālah. 1403/1983

Ibn al-Jawzī. 'Abdur Raḥmān ibn 'Alī ibn Muḥammad. *Ṣifatuṣ Ṣafwah.* Beirūt: Dārul Kitāb al-'Arabī, 1429/2008

Ibn Kathīr, Ismā'īl ibn 'Umar Al-Qurashī Al-Dimashqī *Al-Bidāyah Wan Nihāyah.* Giza: Darul Hijr, 1417/1997

Ibn Khallikān, Abul 'Abbās Shamsuddīn Aḥmad ibn Muḥammad ibn Abī Bakr. *Wafayātul Aa'yān*, Beirūt: Dār Ṣādir, 2005

As Subkī, 'Abdul Wahhāb ibn Ālī ibn 'Abdil Kāfī. *Ṭabaqātush-Shāfi'īyyāh Al-Kubrā.* Dār Iḥyā Al-Kutub Al-'Arabiyyah. 10 vols, 1336/1918

Ibn 'Asākir, *Tārīkh Madīnah Dimishq.* Beirut: Dār al-Fikr, 1415

Al-Qādhi 'Iyāḍ. *Tartībul Madārik Wa Taqrībul Masālik.* Morocco: Wazāratul Awqāf Wash Shuūnul Islāmiyyah. 1403 / 1983

Ibn al-'Imād, Shihābuddīn Muḥammad. *Shadhrātudh Dhahab.* Beirūt: Dār Ibn Kathīr, 1406/1986

At-Talmisānī, Aḥmad ibn Al-Muqrī. Nafḥuṭ Ṭīb Min Ghuṣnil Andalus Ar-Raṭīb. Beirūt: Dār aṣ-Ṣādir, 1408 / 1988

MISCELLANEOUS

Al-Abshīhī. *Al-Mustaṭraf Fī Kullī Fannim Mustaẓraf.* Cairo: Maktabah Al-Jamhūriyyah Al-Arabiyyah, Undated

Al-Ghazālī. Abū Ḥāmid. *Iḥyā' 'Ulūmuddīn.* Cairo: Dār Ash-Shu'b, Undated.

Ar-Rāzi, Muḥammad ibn Amar ibn al-Ḥusain Fakhruddīn. *Manāqib Al-Imām Ash-Shāfi'ī*, Maktabah al-Kulliyyāt al-Azhariyyah, Cairo, 1407 / 1987

Aṣ-Ṣafawī, 'Abdur- Raḥmān ibn 'Abdus Salām ibn 'Uthmān. *Nuzhatul Majālis Wa Muntakhabun Nafā'is.* Cairo: Dārul Bayān al-'Arabī, 1426 / 2005

Al-Yāfi'ī, 'Abdullāh ibn As'ad. *Rowḏur Rayyāḥīn Fī Ḥikāyātiṣ Ṣāliḥīn.* Cairo: Al-Maktabah At-Tawffīqiyyah, undated

Ibn Qudāmah Al-Maqdisī, Abū Muḥammad 'Abdullāh ibn Aḥmad ibn Muḥammad. *Kitābut Tawwābīn.* Beirūt. Mu'assasatur Risālah, 1424 / 2004

Al-Jawzī, Ahmad ibn Muhammad ibn Jajar. *Al Mawā'iẓ Wal Majālis.* Ṭanṭā: Dāruṣ Ṣaḥābah Lit Turāth, 1411 / 1990

Ibn Al-Jawzī, Abul Faraj. *'Uyūnul Ḥikāyāt.* Cairo: Maktabah Fayyāḍ, 1427/2006

Ibn Taymiyah. *Minhāj as-Sunnah An-Nabawiyyah*, 1406 / 1986

At-Tannūkhī, Abī 'Alī al-Muḥsin ibn Abil Qāsim. *Al-Faraj Ba'dash Shiddah.* Cairo: Maktabah Al-Khānjī. 1415/1994

Maktabī, Nadhīr Muḥammad. *Ṣafḥātun Rā'idah Fī Masīratil 'Adālah.* Beirūt: Dārul Bashā'ir. 1419/1998

Aṭ-Ṭartūshī, Muḥammad ibn Walīd al-Fahrī. *Sirājul Mulūk.*

Waṭfah, Hanā. *Al-I'itibār Min Siyaril Abrār.* Beirut: Dārul Ma'rifah, 1428/2007

Al Manshāwī. 'Abdullāh. *Min Qaṣaṣil 'Arab.* Cairo: Maktabatul Īmān, undated

'Imrān, 'Abdul 'Aẓīm. *300 Qissah Wa Qissah Wāqi'iyyah Mu'ath-tharah.* Cairo: Alfan 1430/2010

Muṣṭafā, Usāmah Na'īm. *Anīsul Mu'minīn.* 'Ammān: Dārun Nafāis, 1423/2004

URDU

'Abbāsī, Al-Husn. *Kitābo Kī Darasgāh Me.* Karāchī: Maktabah 'Umar Fārūq, 1427

Al-Damīrī, Kamāluddīn. *Ḥayātul Ḥayawān.* [an Urdu translation of Ḥayātul Ḥayawān]. Deoband: Shams Publishers, 1413 / 1993

Arsalān ibn Akhtar. *Allāh Ke Āshiqo Ke Hālāt.* Karāchī: Maktabah-e-Arsalan, 2006

Ibn Al-Jawzī, Baghdādī. *Laṭā'ife 'Ilmiyya.* [an Urdu translation of Ibn Jawzī's Al-Adhkiyā' by Ishtiyāq Aḥmad]. Karāchī: Dārul Ishā'at, 2002

Bāndwī, Qāri Ṣiddīq Aḥmad. *Ādābul Muta'allimīn.* Bānda: Maktabah Raḥmāniyyah

Fārānī, ʿAbdullāh. *Baro Kā Bachpan.* Multān: Idārah Ta'līfāte Ashrafiyyah, 1430

Naīmuddīn, *Jawāhir Pāre.* Volume 1-3. Lahore: Maktabah Qāsimiyyah, 1426/2005

Qāsimī, Muḥammad Inʿāmul Ḥaq. *Ahle Dil Ke Tarpādene Wāle Wāqiāt.* Delhi: Fareed Book Depot. 1428

Ṣiddīqī, Muḥammad Ḥusain, *Khawātīne Islam Ke Īmān Afroz Wāqiʿāt*, Karachi: Zamzam Publishers. 2006

Pālanpūrī, Yūnus. *Bikhre Motī.* Karāchī: Maktabah Saʿīd Aḥmad Khān, 1424

Surūr, Muḥammad ʿUwais. *Aimmah Arbaʿah Ke Dilchasp Wāqiāt.* Dehli: Arīb Publications, undated

ENGLISH

Kāndhalwī, Muḥammad Zakariyya. *Aap Beti.* [an English translation of Aap Beati]. Dārun Nashrur Raḥmāniyyah, 1428 / 2007

Ash-Shāfiʿī, Muḥammad Ibn Yūsuf Aṣ-Ṣāliḥi Ad-Dimishqī. *Imām Abū Ḥanīfah.* [an English translation of ʿUqūdul Jummān], Azaadeville: Madrasah Arabia Islamia, undated

M

O

P

R

S

T

W

Z

Also from

MUSLIMS AT WORK PUBLICATIONS

Pearls from the Path
Volume 1

A Collection of Anecdotes and Stories from Islamic History

Compiled by Moulānā Afzal Ismail

The Pearl Necklace
A Saint Deceived by the Devil
Graves of Ṣaḥābah ﷺ Opened
Glimpses from the life of ʿUmar ibn ʿAbdul ʿAzīz رحمة الله عليه
A Woman Who Spoke from the Qur'ān for Forty Years
Adventures of a Student of Ḥadīth
Marriages with a Difference
Glimpses from the Life of Imām Bukhārī رحمة الله عليه
The Wisdom of Imām Abū Ḥanīfah رحمة الله عليه
The Daughter of Saʿīd ibn Muṣayyab رحمة الله عليه
Vain Attempt to Steal the Body of Nabī ﷺ
Tears of Ṣalāḥuddīn Ayyūbī رحمة الله عليه *Overpower the Enemy*
Unchallenged Beauty of the Qur'ān
Justice of Islam Wins Hearts
Sacrifice of ʿUlamā' in Pursuit of Knowledge
and many more...

Muslims at Work Publications

Publishers of Islāmic books and

The Muslim Family Magazine

P.O. Box 606, Heidelberg, 1438

South Africa

Website : www.matwork.co.za

Email : info@muslimsatwork.co.za

Tel : +27 73 183 0721